May the Lord g...
you and lead you
into Truth!

Kothi Marai
May 2, 2006

How Can I Come Up?

by

Kozhi Sidney Makai

authorHOUSE™

1663 LIBERTY DRIVE, SUITE 200
BLOOMINGTON, INDIANA 47403
(800) 839-8640
WWW.AUTHORHOUSE.COM

© 2005 Kozhi Sidney Makai. All Rights Reserved.

No part of this book may be reproduced, stored in a retrieval system, or transmitted by any means without the written permission of the author.

First published by AuthorHouse 12/16/05

ISBN: 1-4208-7227-3 (sc)

Printed in the United States of America
Bloomington, Indiana

This book is printed on acid-free paper.

All scriptures are in the King James Version except where otherwise noted.

Praise for the Book

"...deep....and...truthful. It makes you "wake up and smell" the coffee. It's inspiring and motivational."
- Charity Sodala, Management Trainee, African Banking Corporation, Zambia, Africa

"I must confess it has been...one of the most powerful motivational sources of information to have fallen in my hands in many a month. The definition of the word imagination really blew me away. I believe this book will be a very strong and resourceful motivational tool..."
- Pastor Alex Phiri, Milton Keynes, United Kingdom

"Great examples of what happens when we do only 99% instead of our all on our jobs, etc... I truly appreciate all of these "life lessons" especially for teaching children. The Lord expects us to do our best at all times and these are tremendous reminders."
- Joey Chandler, Director of Undergraduate Admissions, Sam Houston State University, Huntsville, Texas

"I think this book eloquently summarizes a philosophy given to me by my parents, "Be steadfast in faith, strong in character, and true to all around you." If nothing else is gained from reading the book, it reiterates the important tenet of making the most of what God gives you."
- Stefanie Dugan Lowe, Administrative Services Manager, City of Oakland Public Works Agency, Oakland, California

"This is a thought - provoking piece to guide us in practically all aspects of our lives. It is a very refreshing way to spur us into action. The author practices what he was preaching by being an initiator rather than an imitator..."
- Dr. David Sam, President, North Harris College, Houston, Texas

"The words of encouragement from this book were medicine to my soul. Today was a challenging day to say the least. However, after reading chapter eight on desire, my soul feels revived. The message is clear: stay persistent."

- Tyron Coleman, President, Premier Mortgage Lending Services & Coleman's Financial Services, Houston, Texas

"Kozhi Makai's book contains nuggets for daily living that can truly make a difference!
Discipline that is applied with diligence and mercy (both for us and towards others!) is an important skill to learn. Kozhi shows you how to gain insights developing discipline and other skills to improve your life!

- Dr. Ruth Achterhof, Faculty member at Baker College, Jones International University, Davenport University, and the United Nations Development Program (UNDP) Virtual Academy

"Kozhi has done a wonderful job of expressing himself and encouraging others to be all that they can be!"

- Johnny Green, Senior Pastor, Connextions Church, Cyfair, Texas

"...quality work...I can honestly say I was deeply moved *and* inspired. It speaks tremendous truth and honesty to empower people not only to "focus on the positive and not dwell on the negative" but also to take whatever circumstances one is given and make the absolute best of it all while maintaining your dreams."

- Tim Carlisle, President, Woodlands Christian Athletic Association (WCAA), The Woodlands, Texas

Dedication

This book is first dedicated to my friend, Lord, and savior, Jesus Christ – the Anointing. Without You Lord, where would I be? I am capable because you were culpable; what can I say? You're what every guy like me needs: a true friend.

This book is the product of a conversation with Gregory "Skippy" Kapeleula. It is to you, next, that I dedicate this book. I hope that I have now answered that question you asked me a few years ago. Sorry I took so long...

This book is also dedicated to all those who want to come up. Spread those wings!

Acknowledgments

Seeing that I have already acknowledged my friend and the Lover of my Soul, Jesus, I would like to acknowledge the following individuals and organizations:

- Annie Makai, my bride and pride; though this book was envisioned and mainly written before we began our journey together, you have been the source of great strength. I was a boy and have now become a man because of your love.
- Timothy Vowell, my friend, colleague and writing consultant; this book would not be complete had you not spent countless hours advising me and helping me learn from your mistakes.
- Tamara Ohlson, my editor; so, for a young woman straight out of college, you have done pretty well! We had to push each other for this project to be completed and now we are done – we have become the blessing!
- Elizabeth Harper, my proof reader; I am thankful, first, that I am almost the one person that can call you Liz and get away with it! You have put in so much time into this product and I thank you for your loyalty and dedication to the cause of Christ.
- Dr. Ron & Rev. Tonia Woolever, "one" set of my parents in the Lord; thanks for all the wonderful comments and suggestions. I appreciate you both so much.
- George & Renee Eberly, my friends and parents; thank you for loving me despite my pitfalls. Words cannot quantify the love and honor I have for you!
- Spring Tabernacle, my Bible college & church; the ministry and every single member of Spring Tabernacle is responsible, in part, for the ideas presented in this book.
- AuthorHouse Publishing, especially Miss Nancy Szylakowski, thank you all for working with me and providing me an avenue to share my heart with the world. You've won yourselves a faithful friend and endorser

- Finally, my pastor, Bishop C.G. "Jabo" Green; regardless of the circumstances, you have provided me with an example worth following. When I moved to the United States and we met, you may not have realized that you had inherited diversity into your family; your favorite Zambian son! Thank you for all the talks and the direction leading up to this publication.

Contents

Forward

Kozhi Makai is a remarkable young man. I truly believe him to be one of the "young lions" we often read about, who will help change the face of the future. He is a "spiritual son" whom I love deeply but have very little time to be with face-to-face. Yet, I know his heart. I know his passion to fulfill his destiny and to become one of the change-makers who will change the future of his country. Also, I know Kozhi desires to be the man that his God has called him to be.

After more than thirty years of ministry – preaching, teaching, counseling and motivating people to grow – I've read more than my share of self-help, motivating-type books. Consequently, it was with a slight degree of skepticism that I began this book. Yet before ending the first chapter, I realized that I held a real jewel in my hands. In an age where we are all too busy and weary of reading many books, Kozhi has done us all a wonderful service: he has fed abundantly on the words of other authors and distilled for us a powerful drink of wisdom in one concise volume.

Yes, How Can I Come Up? is a "self-help" book; yet, it is much more. While it challenges the reader to unlock the potential hidden within his heart, it also reveals that such a goal cannot be attained without the help of the Creator of all mankind.

In the first chapter, Kozhi sets the tone by establishing Adam and Eve as people called to succeed, not two people who simply failed and were forgotten. Kozhi weaves the truth of Biblical teachings throughout this book. He ultimately challenges the reader to stop dwelling upon his failures and to look beyond the circumstances he may be in and raise his eyes to a God who created him to be more than a conqueror. Kozhi has successfully challenged us to walk hand-in-hand with God and become "all we've been called to be."

I highly recommend How Can I Come Up? to all who know that life has much more to offer and are willing to go for it.

Dr. Ron Woolever
Shammah Ministries International
Azle, Texas

Preface

I was in Houston, Texas, when a friend asked me the question "How can I come up?" This was after we had had a conversation concerning my own "come up." My friend moved to the United States almost three years before I did, and yet I seemed to have "passed him" in only a year and a half. "How can I come up?" was his way of asking how he could succeed in life and prosper in *all* of his endeavors. That question is the impetus for this publication.

There are many people in our world today that are seeking a way to be more productive and successful in life. Success, be it financial, spiritual, or interpersonal, is the talk of many tongues. Everyone wants to get their hands on their share of success, but disillusionment and lack of understanding seem to draw them further and further away from it. There have been numerous books written about the "keys" to success throughout the history of mankind; though most have cited researched methods and practices, there is one that remains untapped – the Biblical model. The underlying principle of this book is that mankind is endowed with the seeds of greatness as bestowed by God:

> And God blessed them, and God said unto them, Be fruitful, and multiply, and replenish the earth, and subdue it and have dominion over the fish of the sea, and over the fowl of the air, and over every living thing that moveth upon the earth – Genesis 1:28, King James Version

Why is it, then, that man carries on as though he is not part of the Divine Equation? This question, and others like it, are what you and I will probe so that by the end of this reading, you will have found the principle ingredients and the baking instructions for your own pie of success; and you will never again ask "How can I come up?"

KOZHI SIDNEY MAKAI
The Woodlands, Texas
January 2005

Introduction

Success is not measured by how you do compared to what somebody else does; success is measured by how you do compared to what you could have done with the ability you have – Zig Ziglar

In today's world of E-Commerce and the World Wide Web, everyone is trying to maximize profits and increase efficiency – thereby, trying to be a success. The principle of responsibility is central to the idea of success. Responsibility comes from the root word *respond* which simply means "to make answer." Most people that are trying to be successful fail because they are not making answers for themselves and what they are doing. Success is a *personal* responsibility, and cannot be handed down or blamed on another entity; the responsibility is yours, and yours alone!

Success is getting up in the morning and not being able to tell the difference between what you have to do and what you want to do - Sandy Deabler

Success has a variety of definitions, and one that truly impressed me was offered by Sandy Deabler, a psychology professor of almost fifteen years at North Harris College in Houston, Texas. She said that success is getting up in the morning and not being able to tell the difference between what you have to do and what you want to do. To this she added, "If you love what you do and do what you love, I think you're successful." I also believe, however, the words I saw in an office that said: *Success is a journey, not a destination.* How true that is! God created us for success, and as such it ought to be a perpetual aspect of our lives. Success should be looked at as a "process of achievement." Achievers are always looking for ways to succeed; hence they are always challenging themselves. I heard it once said that high achievers shoot for the stars; if they fall short of their mark, at least they come back with stardust in their hands. Are you an achiever? Noticed any stardust lately?

Success in any area of life isn't something you do; rather, it's something to see. Success is an understanding, not an activity - W. Clement Stone

Success is a lot of things to a lot of people. I love W. Clement Stone's definition of success. He says, "Success in any area of life isn't something you do; rather, it's something to see. Success is an understanding, not an activity." Judging from the definitions thus far quoted, I feel that it is safe to say that success is not an outward event but a spiritual or internal event. It is tragically comic to see those that are *not* financially secure or "successful" painting an outward picture to that effect. Most people that actually are financially secure or successful are hardly as extravagant as those that only paint the picture of being so. Success *must* be "spiritual" and internal before the human eye can see it. I say this because it must "occur" in one's subconscious before it can manifest itself in one's corporeal world.

I have asked several people how they define success, and some of the responses I have received have been truly remarkable. However, success is like most passwords – it is case-sensitive! In other words, success is whatever *you* think it should be: One man's food is another man's poison. My brothers in Hong Kong eat frogs, my brothers in the United States eat crabs, but each may lose their appetite at the sight of a caterpillar called *chinkubala* or termite called *Inswa* that the natives of Zambia eat. Whatever the case may be, what one individual perceives as success may not be regarded as such by another individual.

While walking towards my car one semester after an exam, a credit card solicitor asked me to fill out an application and offered to give me a free t-shirt when I was finished. Motivated by the shirt and inclined to help this young lady, I agreed to this five minute ordeal. While I was filling out the paperwork, she asked me something and I unknowingly told her that I had quite a hard test and was ready to go home. Her response was, "Well, you passed it at least." I told her I had, but then asked her whether that was the point. You see, to her, if she passed the test it was good enough, but for me it was not good enough to just *pass* a test. It was at this moment that a glorious revelation was given to me. I realized that success is not for the ordinary. It is not for the normal. Success is for the extraordinary – those who dare to go beyond the confines of their minds and scope.

I cannot hold it against someone if his or her life-long dream is to be a janitor. For whatever reason, that is success to them. I have no less respect for a janitor than I do for a CEO of a Fortune 500 company. The essence of what I am trying to say is that it is meaningless to live below your potential. I also wish for you to understand that you have to define success in your *own* terms before you start the journey. I am convinced that many take the wrong road not because they are unaware that it does not lead to success, but because they do not know what success is. You see, if you do not know where you're going, any road will lead you there.

Success is the ability to choose one way over another – it provides options
– Kozhi Sidney Makai

Having come from a humble beginning and background, my definition of success is unlike what has been discussed thus far: Success is the ability to choose one way over another – it provides options. A "successful" man has the option of eating lobster, steak, or hamburgers. An "unsuccessful" man, however, has no option but to eat rice and beans. Being from a Developing Nation, I learned very quickly that my options were limited. Indeed, I had more options than most, but I still did not have much choice in where I went to school and what I studied. Success affords people the options to choose where they go to school, what and where they eat, and what they study. Success can be financial, spiritual or intellectual. In any area of success, ability is key. Ability is simply the "power to do one thing over another."

There is one very important question that must be asked before any endeavor towards success is pursued: *Who am I?* This is an age-old question that has constantly puzzled men, women and children across the world and throughout the annals of history. In the quest to find and define themselves, many people have turned to ungodly sources such as drugs, alcohol, and premarital or extramarital sex. Any man, woman or child that honestly knows who they are is already on his or her way to success and prosperity.

I will praise thee; for I am fearfully and wonderfully made
– Psalms 139:14

Despite what you may have heard, read or said before now, you are God's child, fearfully and wonderfully made as the psalmist wrote. Born into His royal family, you have been given the gifts to improve yourself constantly; the true realization of this is much more satisfying than riches or gold. One of the reasons that we have lack and poverty in our world today is that many people have not truly tried to define who they are. Before one can truly pursue success, one must first define *who* one is. In defining oneself, there are many questions that must be answered – and answered honestly. A man's intellectual and spiritual completeness is closer to fruition once he is able to be honest with himself. I once read a most intriguing quote that read:

You may be like Jack Horner and chisel a plum

And you think you're a wonderful guy

But the man in the glass says you're only a bum

If you can't look him straight in the eye

Simply put, there is no way one can truly succeed and become "all he can be" without first being honest with himself. This honesty with oneself will make it highly unlikely for one to be dishonest with another man.

Success isn't due to luck or chance. Real success is a matter of finding yourself and building upon what you find

Every gift or desire is first born in one's spirit. Robert Browning, the 19th century poet wrote that "when a man's fight begins within himself, he is worth something." It is clear from this quote that greatness does not begin anywhere but within. You cannot find out who you truly are if you are constantly battling against yourself. Dr. Martin Luther King meditated on this point when he said, "Stand up! Because a man cannot ride your back unless it's bent over." It is all about *you* when it comes to what you *allow* to happen *within* you. We are all stirred up in anger or in love, but what matters most is how we react to that stirring. One must have at least a spark in order to start the fire of success. Carol Moseley Braun, America's first black female senator, said, "You cannot blaze forth unless the fire has been smoldered within you." Now, I have no doubt in my mind that Senator Brown had been planning her ascent to the U.S Senate long before she blazed forth into the political arena, and eventually the Senate, making history along the way. *Is the fire smoldering within you?*

The secret of success is constancy to purpose – Benjamin Disraeli, Speech at the Crystal Palace June 24, 1870

By way of the world, the enemy has tried to find ways to prevent you from regarding yourself as what you truly are: God's *child* – fearfully and wonderfully made – and His *special creation*. You were born into a royal family, and the faster you realize that God wants nothing but the best for you, the faster your "come up" will come into fruition. If you focus on God, refusing to work according to the ways of this world, you will find success and prosperity in the Spirit and in your finances, and in all other facets of your life as well.

You have to ask yourself who you are. And when you do, which answer are you going to accept? The one that tells you that you are God's child and His special creation or are you going to believe what the world says?

As science loves to state, you are nothing but a mixture of common chemicals, mostly water (enough to fill a small bathtub) and fat (enough to produce four or five bars of soap). It is also said that there's enough calcium in your body to make a large piece of chalk, enough phosphorus to ignite a pack of matches, enough sodium to season a bag of popcorn, enough magnesium to spark a flashbulb, enough iron to manufacture a three-inch nail, enough iodine to make a child seethe in pain, and enough sulfur to rid a dog of fleas. In total, you're worth two Dollars of water, fat and chemicals. What do *you* think?

Don't make the mistake of looking in the wrong places to find out who you are. Look instead to God. Why lean on mere mortals, when you can have the authentic counsel of Jesus Christ Himself? True, honest soul-searching is truly variable and ranges from depressed to mentally imbalanced or completely sane and hungry for success. Whatever the findings may be, it is very important for one to know whether one has a problem that needs to be dealt with. The one way to do this is to search deep within oneself and to be honest with what you fnd.

It's hard to be a star when your skills ain't up to par;
It's hard to push a lex when you don't even own a car;
It's hard to win the battle when you can't win this war;
It's hard to be a man when you don't know who you are

I came across these words while listening to a Christian rap/R & B group called *KJ-52 and Sons of Intellect*. What wise words! How *can* you honestly expect to drive a *Lexus* when you don't even own a car? Many people do not realize that success, and indeed life, is about process – what the philosophers of religion, and process theologians, call *causality*. A seed *must* be planted for a harvest to take place. So it is with success – you can't be a man unless you know who you are!

Chapter One

The blessing of the Lord, it maketh rich, and He addeth no sorrow with it
— Proverbs 10:12

The Old Testament book of Joshua begins with the divine appointment of Joshua by God in which Joshua is told that, because Moses is dead, he is to lead the children of Israel to the Promised Land, and that as long as he keeps God's Word, he will be successful (Joshua 1:1-9, King James Version). This is the only place in the early English versions of the Bible where the word "success" is found. In the Hebrew text, the word used for success is "sakal[1]," pronounced *saw-kal*. The literal translation is "to be circumspect and hence intelligent," or simply, "wisdom." Success is not the BMW or Rolls Royce that we see "successful" men and women drive! The expensive car is only a *manifestation* of success. All too often we base our notion of success upon the outward appearance of those whom we feel are successful. In essence, what God is telling Joshua is, "I have empowered you with the ability and seeds of greatness."

Webster's dictionary defines success as "the termination or result of any affair, whether happy or unhappy[2]." Using this definition, it is quite easy to see that success is only a *manifestation* or *termination* of an affair.

The same Hebrew word – "*sakal*" – is also used for "prosper." Therefore, being prosperous is having the intelligence and wisdom to *produce* the manifestation of the fruits of prosperity. Webster defines "prosper" in several ways, but one that catches my attention is the definition: "to thrive[3]." Where there is thriving, there is abundance. Therefore, this clearly negates the secular, and often Christian, mentality that Christians should live on "E."

During my teenage years in Zambia, it was quite a luxury for us as young men to drive (our parents' cars); let alone, to have a gas tank on "F" (full tank). When we did have a car, we always traveled on enough – "E." This is the very same mentality that many Christians carry. At one point in my life, I thought that all preachers and priests were supposed to be poor because it was pious. It wasn't until I began to study the Word deeper and more intently that I realized that prosperity is but a fruit of something that is endowed to me *just because I am a child of God.*

The Garden of Eden, Adam and Eve's home, was filled with riches and prosperity:

And the Lord planted a garden eastward in Eden; and there
he put the man who he had formed. And out of the ground
made the Lord God to grow every tree that is pleasant to
the sight, and good for food; the tree of life also in the
midst of the garden, and the tree of knowledge of good
and evil. And a river went out of Eden to water the garden;
and from thence it was parted and became four heads. The
name of the first is Pison; that is it which compasseth the
whole land of Havilah, where there is gold. And the gold
of that land is good; there is bdellium and the onyx stone.
And the name of the second river is Gihon; the same is
it that compasseth the whole land of Ethiopia. And the
name of the third river is Hiddekel; that is it, which goeth
toward the east of Assyria. And the fourth is the Euphrates.
– Genesis 2:8-14 KJV

Pardon my asking but is it difficult to see that Adam and Eve were
successful and prosperous? First, the land they occupied was filled
with the purest gold and most precious of stones. Furthermore, there
were four tributaries running through the garden and the soil was
unmistakably rich and fertile. From the beginning God intended for
man to be prosperous and successful in all his dealings. Deal with it!

HOW TRADITIONS IMPEDE SUCCESS

The Master, sick of the hypocritical Pharisees, said that the traditions
of men often nullify the Word of God (Mark 7:13). I have learned that
a lot of the customs and conventions that were passed down to me
during my formative years as a young boy were wrong! For example,
living in Africa, I would have absolutely lost my mind if a black cat
crossed my path! Once, I made the mistake of wearing a red shirt while
riding my bike in the neighborhood, and when it began thundering
and lightning, I jumped off my bike and lay flat-faced on the ground
because I had been told that lightning strikes those who wear red.

It is imperative to remove our slave mentality (for once we
were slaves of sin) and see the Word and Kingdom of God for what
it is. Paul wrote: "the Kingdom of God is not meat and drink; but

righteousness, peace and joy in the Holy Ghost" (Romans 14:17). And in his first letter to the Corinthians, he wrote: "The Kingdom of God is not in word but in power" (1 Corinthians 4:20). There is freedom in the Kingdom of God and we must sanctify ourselves by renewing our minds daily.

Having already introduced Adam and Eve as being a wealthy and prosperous couple, let us now turn and examine the nature and the characteristics of the first two humans. In Genesis we read that God conferred with and within Himself, and decided to make man in His own image. "So God created man in His own image, in the image of God created He him; male and female created He them" (Genesis 1:27). What He did next is the most profound and prolific thing to be done for man since his conception...

A literary analysis of Genesis 1 reveals some of the best poetry in the Hebrew Bible. "And God said..." is the beginning of some of the most incredible and moving poetry at the couplet level. All the way to verse 28, we have a narrative that is rhythmical and ordered. Then God speaks the first words to His new creation, humanity...

> "And God blessed them, and God said unto them,
> Be fruitful, and multiply, and replenish the earth, and
> subdue it. And have dominion over the fish of the sea,
> and over the fowl of the air, and over every living thing
> that moveth upon the earth." (Genesis 1:28 KJV)

This verse struck me as odd because, though it is not in the "And God said..." poetic form, it follows through with the concept of endowment. When God said, "Let there be..." He begins to grant endowments to what He created. He endowed light with its ability to "overshadow" darkness and govern the day. He endowed the stars and moon with the ability to govern the night. Land animals were endowed with the ability to live on dry land, and vegetation is given the ability to grow in the soil.

However, with humanity, God blesses them, thus giving them the natural capability and ability to be fruitful, and to multiply, and to replenish the earth, to subdue it, and to have dominion. What's wrong with that picture? I thought the Christian man was supposed to be begging for bread, broke and looking shabby because it is pious? God made this world for man to rule and enjoy while He sits in Heaven and presides there. So, how many rulers do you know that beg for bread, are broke and look shabby? So why should we?

THE SEED

Aside from a few exceptions in the Old Testament, wherever one sees the word "blessed," the Hebrew word corresponding to it is *barak*[4], pronounced *baw-rak*. *Barak* simply means "to praise, congratulate, salute or thank." My question is: What does God have to congratulate humanity for? Let's go deeper…

What God does, in essence, is give humans the authority to rule, and the provisions to do so. When He says, "be fruitful," He is not *asking* us to be fruitful, multiply, replenish, subdue and have dominion – He is *commanding* us to! Because it is a command, it seems to me almost treasonous not to obey.

Dr. Creflo Dollar once said, "The blessing is the root of the fruit[5]." How right he was! See, you can't get any fruit without a root. You can't get any roots without any seed. A seed is defined by Webster as: "The impregnated and matured ovule of a plant, containing an embryo, which may be developed, and converted into an individual similar to that from which it derives its origin[6]." Wow! Where does humanity derive its origin? Yes, sir! From God Almighty! Yahweh! Elohim! The Most High God!

I, therefore, have no choice but to be like that from which I derive my existence or origin – Elohim! When a seed is planted, the first thing to shoot out is the root. Once the root is entrenched then out comes the shoot, and eventually the plant bears fruit. Success is like this: one must first be rooted and hidden before the shoot and fruit can be seen.

In the above definition, a seed is described as being *impregnated*. Likened unto man, what are we impregnated or endowed with? The ability to succeed! Dr. Creflo Dollar says that to be blessed is to be "empowered to have success[7]."

The blessing will always *precede* fruitfulness, multiplication, replenishment, subjugation, and subsequent dominion. Many begin their walk with God on a very sour note because they do not truly believe in their salvation in the first place. If they truly believed in it, they would not walk with hearts laden with guilt, feelings of impotence and lack. I used to feel very inadequate when it came to the matters of my salvation. With each altar call, I found myself on my knees begging God to save me. Like a seed, I was impregnated but was not mature and could produce no fruit. Such lack of maturity almost inevitably produces worry and faithlessness.

SEEK THE KINGDOM FIRST

The Master, upon seeing the multitudes, went up a mountain and began to teach:

> Therefore, I say unto you, take no thought for your life, what ye shall eat, or what ye shall drink; nor yet for your body, what ye shall put on. Is not the life more than meat, and the body than raiment? Behold the fowls of the air, for they sow not, neither do they reap, nor gather into barns, yet your Heavenly Father feedeth them. Are ye not much better than they? Which of you by taking thought can add one cubit unto his stature? And why take ye thought for raiment? Consider the lilies of the field, how they grow; they toil not, neither do they spin. And yet I say unto you that even Solomon in all his glory was not arrayed like one of these. Wherefore, if God so clothe the grass of the field, which today is and tomorrow is cast into the oven, shall He not much more clothe you, O ye of little faith? Therefore, take not thought, saying, 'What shall we eat?' or 'What shall we drink?' or 'Wherewithal shall we be clothed?' for after these things do the Gentiles seek. For your Heavenly Father knoweth that ye have need of these things. But seek ye first the kingdom of God and His righteousness, and all these things shall be added unto you. Take therefore no thought for the morrow, for the morrow shall take thought for the things of itself. Sufficient unto the day is the evil thereof. (Matthew 6:25-34)

I believe that, second to rebellion, *theodicy*, the questioning of God's justice, is the worst thing that any sensible Christian can attempt to do. Ask Job, He found out pretty quickly that "the secret things belong unto the Lord our God; but the revealed belong unto us and to our children forever, that we may do all the words of this law" (Deuteronomy 29:29). The Master said we are to seek the Kingdom of God and His righteousness first, and then all these "things" would be added unto us. See, the blessing is the *architect* of the manifestation. Once the blessing is in order and in place, it is free to draw up plans and start construction!

The Kingdom of God? What's that? Webster defines a kingdom as "the state or territory ruled by a king[8]." If the Kingdom of God is seen in this way, then the Master was no more than an agent for a new political dynasty – a Zealot! The Master spoke Aramaic. The Gospel, like the rest of the New Testament, was written in Greek. The Greek word for kingdom is *basileia*; which more often means the *activities* of a king rather than the territory he rules. The Aramaic word for kingdom is *malkutha*; which certainly has that meaning (activities of a king). Thus the Master was talking about what we might call the *kingship* of God rather than His kingdom. The Master used "kingdom" to refer to the *relationship* of the king (God) with His people; the inner workings of the kingdom. Therefore, the possession of righteousness and of the kingdom precludes fruitfulness, multiplication, replenishment, subjugation and domination. A preacher that once visited our church defined righteousness as the common sense of God. Hence we must entreat God to bestow common sense on us, and then we can have dominion.

THE FRUIT

In the first "commandment," God implores His children to be fruitful, multiply, replenish the earth, subdue it, and have dominion. To better understand the implications and ramifications of this bidding, we need to know what each word means. Webster's dictionary defines *fruitful* as: "prolific, producing or presenting in abundance[9];" *multiply* as: "to add to itself any given number of times or to increase in number[10];"

replenish as: "to stock with numbers or abundance[11];" *subdue* as: "to conquer and bring into subjection[12];" and *dominion* as: "sovereign or supreme authority[13]."

There is a sequence in attaining the fruit of the blessing. And what is the fruit of the blessing? Sovereign and supreme authority! It couldn't come from any other set of lips than the Most High, Elohim. The fruitfulness, multiplication, replenishment, and subjugation all culminate into supreme and sovereign authority. Authority over one's life, authority over one's family, authority over one's finances, you name it.

In order to attain the fruit, you must first grow in *knowledge* of the Word (be fruitful), then you can multiply in *wisdom*, being sure to stock and retain that wisdom so that you are able to conquer and bring into subjection the principalities and powers that try to deny you access to your sovereign authority. Once each of these steps is completed, you will be able to reign with divine authority.

Abide in me, and I in you; as the branch cannot bear fruit of itself except it abide in the vine. No more can ye, except ye abide in me. I am the vine, ye are the branches; he that abideth in me, and I in him, the same bringeth forth much fruit; for without me ye can do nothing. John 15:4-5

It is absolutely impossible for a branch to bear fruit without being connected to the vine. You see, the branch is endowed with the power to bear fruit as long as it is connected to or abides in the vine. The blessing flows from the root, through the vine, and to the branch. Without the vine, the empowerment is severed.

The Master taught that *the branch cannot bear fruit of itself except it abide in the vine.* Sometimes the Christian will get into the "woe is me" attitude and completely forget that the first page of the Bible (depending on font size) endows him or her with the seeds of success. This "woe is me" attitude is the beginning of separation from the vine. Get this into your frame of mind: The branch cannot bear fruit of itself. Remember, presumption is the forerunner of a great fall.

"Ye are the salt of the earth; but if the salt have lost his savor, wherewithal shall it be salted? It is henceforth good for nothing but to be cast out and to be trodden under foot of men. Ye are the light of the world. A city that is set on an hill cannot be hid. Neither do men light a candle, and put it under a bushel; but on a candlestick and it giveth light unto all that are in the house. Let your light so shine before men, that they may see your good works, and glorify your Father, which is in heaven."
Matthew 5:13-16

In ancient Israel, salt was used to season food. This seasoning was also a manner of preservation. What the Master is saying to us is that we are supposed to be an example, through preservation of His ways, and a light in this dark world. Unfortunately, we have made Christianity unattractive to unbelievers because we live a make-believe and hypocritical life of foolish piety.

I remember when one of Zambia's most anointed and spectacular ministers, Nevers Mumba, returned from the United States and set the airwaves on fire with charismatic and empowered preaching. The man was truly anointed by God and was living in a very large, beautiful home. There was much talk and murmuring because, to us, preachers shouldn't be living "so extravagantly." What I, and perhaps many other Zambians at that time, did not know or realize was that it was not his fault that the blessings of God had now matured into dominion. How could he preach credibly about God's provision if he himself was living in a little hole in the back of nowhere?

The Master taught that if salt loses its savor, it is good for nothing but to be trodden under foot of men. Guess what? The Christian is being trodden under foot of men because of foolish piety. The Master went on to say in the same chapter that "except your righteousness shall exceed the righteousness of the scribes and Pharisees, ye shall in no case enter into the kingdom of heaven" (Matthew 5:20). Today, most of the "church folks" aren't upset at the secular bands and singers because that is a voice that the Lord can use; they're mad because these singers and bands *done came up financially and they're jealous*! The body of

Christ today is full of hypocrisy and foolish piety, and that mentality has got to go!

The candle is empowered by its maker and by its nature to give light. The Christian is empowered by his original nature and his Creator to shine before men, so that others may see his good works and glorify God. It is quite hard to shine and show good works wearing a hand-me-down suit, hand-me-down gold tooth, and shoes borrowed from Uncle Joe! It's time for the Christian Church to wake up and smell the coffee!

Chapter Two

I beseech you, therefore, brethren, by the mercies of God, that ye present your bodies a living sacrifice, holy, acceptable unto God, which is your reasonable service. And be not conformed to this world but be ye transformed by the renewing of your mind, that ye may prove what is that good, and acceptable, and perfect will of God – Romans 12:1-2

There was an eagle that lost an egg one day and, as fate would have it, the tiny eagle egg was found by a hen. She took the egg home to the chicken coop and sat on it with all the loving patience of an incipient mother. A few weeks later the egg was hatched, and out stepped a tiny eagle. The tiny bird had an eagle history, eagle genes, eagle chromosomes, eagle power, and eagle potential. But because he was born into a chicken environment, he grew up thinking he was a chicken. He grew up dreaming chicken dreams and thinking chicken thoughts and playing chicken games and entertaining chicken ambitions.

He was, in fact, made to feel ashamed of his eagle features. You see, even though he didn't know who he was, the other birds in the barnyard did. They met among themselves and said, "We've got to keep this bird thinking that he's a chicken, because if he ever finds out that he's an eagle, he'll rule over us."

As a result, the little bird became ashamed of his eagle heritage and eagle features. The other birds made fun of his mighty eagle beak, because they had little thin, narrow, weak chicken beaks. They also made fun of his mighty eagle talons, because they possessed weak, tiny, scrawny chicken feet. And he became ashamed of the richness of his deep, dark eagle feathers. At one point in his life, he even considered cosmetic surgery. He thought about cutting off half of his eagle beak and dyeing his dark eagle feathers, so he could look more like the chickens. Ironically, his greatest ambition in life was to one day hop, skip, and jump up on the fence post to cockle-doodle-do at daybreak like the rooster.

But one day, when this confused bird was playing in the barnyard, he saw the deep dark contours of a mighty shadow swim across the ground. For the first time in his life, this little lost bird looked higher than the fence post, higher that the tree line, and saw

12

the remarkable sight of an adult eagle in full flight – with all of its majesty, grace, and power. The little lost bird was transfixed. He said to himself, "Wow! I sure wish I could be like that."

The adult eagle perceived the dilemma of the little lost bird and swooped down from the stratospheric heights and said, "Boy, you ain't no chicken. You're an eagle! Your mighty talons were not meant to rake and scrape on the ground for worms or feed, but to snatch the craggy side of yonder mountain of achievement."

"Boy," he repeated, "You ain't no chicken. You're an eagle! Your eagle eye was not meant to be limited to the narrow confines of the barnyard but to seek out the distant horizon of your own unfulfilled potential, and spread your wings as you catch the lofty winds of your immeasurable genius. You ain't no chicken – you're an eagle[1]!"

The mind is its own place, and in itself can make a heaven of hell, a hell of heaven – John Milton, Paradise Lost

Because of the traditions of men, and indeed your mindset, instead of being the eagle that you are supposed to be, you have confined yourself to the chicken coop that the enemy and your so-called friends have deceivingly told you is the best you will ever do. So you lie there, in a spiritual and financial limbo, with your chicken thoughts and your chicken dreams when you can soar above and beyond the mediocrity of the chicken coop.

Perhaps the most misused, unused, and abused seed God has given us is our mind. The brain, in itself, is not our mind; it is rather, the dwelling place of the mind and is "a priceless resource that is given to each of us free at birth[2]." We are back to the endowment principle again. I have learned from all my travel that man is prone to find the most sophisticated excuses for lack in his life. When I was younger and tried to make excuses, my parents always told me that a bad carpenter always blames his tools.

The Apostle Paul, writing to his Roman church, expressed the need for the church members to present themselves as living sacrifices unto God, because that was their reasonable service. He went on to add that the Church needed to renew its mind daily so it could prove (discern) what the good, acceptable and perfect will of God was (Romans 12:1-2). The key, however, was for the Church to be *transformed* by the *renewing* of its mind.

Transformation cannot be possible without the renewing of the mind since "once we were slaves of unrighteousness, but now we are slaves of righteousness" (Romans 6:16-23). The only way we can understand that we are now slaves to righteousness is to break away from our old mode of thinking and adopt a new way of thinking in Christ Jesus. Too many people are broke in the Church today, and it can be attributed to the fact that they cannot change the way that they think.

John Milton, in his epic <u>Paradise Lost</u>, said, "The mind is its own place, and in itself can make a heaven of hell, a hell of heaven." How true it is! When God begins to move in our lives in unexpected abundance, we wince because we are afraid of what the folks in the Church will think about us. On the other hand, when God does not seem to be moving in our lives with expected abundance, we cry out and complain, basing our prayers on the way He is moving in Sister Rosie's or Brother John's lives.

Ye ask, and receive not, because ye ask amiss, that ye may consume it upon your lusts – James 4:3

A "woe is me" attitude seems to pervade Christian life today. Interestingly, the biggest problem with that "woe is me" attitude is the *me*. God is tired of hearing selfish and lustful prayers from churches and children He has endowed with "all spiritual blessings in heavenly places in Christ" (Ephesians 1:3). The Apostle James wrote that we ask and do not receive because we ask amiss, trying to get it for ourselves. There is no room for selfishness in the Kingdom of God – it's time to leave the "bless-me club!"

When I moved to the United States several years ago, I had nothing: no car, no home, no money and no power. I had no job; I was living in a car, and was hurting financially, socially, and spiritually. The only thing that kept my head above the water was the little faith I had. I used to walk about a mile and a half to the Roman Catholic Church on Aldine Westfield in Spring, Texas, just so I could find solace in the house of the Lord. However, this was not the plan God had for me. If God will not have His children begging bread in the streets, surely He will not have them begging bread in *His house*! And therein was a revelation that changed my walk with the Lord dramatically: I began to seek *God* rather than His blessings. The short end of that story is that the blessing was developed enough to warrant me to be fruitful, to multiply and to replenish. I have a car that was given to me, a place I call home, a family and a closer walk with the Lord. Now I am subduing and having dominion over my mind. You see, Genesis 1:28 is telling us to subdue and have dominion first *over our minds* and then we can conquer and reign in all other areas of our lives.

The real seat of taste is not the tongue but the mind – Mohandas "Mahatma" Gandhi

So, how does one renew one's mind? To equip ourselves with the power to do so, let us begin by understanding the meaning of "renew". The Greek word for it is *anakainosis*[3], pronounced, *an-ak-ahee-no-sis*. It is derived from the word *anakainoo*, which means "to renovate or renew." *Anakainosis* is used only twice in the New Testament, and in each case signifies a *perpetual* process. In Titus 3:5, it is used to signify the "renewing of the Holy Ghost" that God has done in us, so that "we should be made heirs according to the hope of eternal life" (Titus 3:7).

Webster's dictionary defines renew as "to restore to former freshness, completeness, or perfection." Going back to Genesis 1:28, the first thing that God did was to make humanity perfect, then He blessed them, thus endowing them with the ability for success, and then charged them to utilize that endowment. This, friend, is the state of perfection that renewing our minds takes us back to. We begin to realize the potential within ourselves and develop the ability to discern the good, and acceptable, and perfect will of God.

The Fathers goal, which must become our goal, is nothing less than Christlikeness, where we become fully trained in the knowledge of the ways of God ~ Francis Frangipane

The Master taught: "He that believeth on Me, the works that I do shall he do also; and greater works than these shall he do; because I go unto My Father" (John 14:12). What works did the Master do? He healed the sick, blessed the cursed, raised the dead and obeyed the Father. Equally, if we are to walk in the success of our Lord, we will have to be committed to His ways.

In order for us to be a spiritual success, we must take on the likeness of Christ. There is absolutely no way anyone can "come up" without Jesus. Some seem to have done so but that success will be short lived because they are not connected to the True Vine – Jesus Christ.

The Father's goal is for us to be like Christ. The net result of our renewing our mind is bringing us into the ways of the Lord. If Christ is to be our example, what mind are we to have? The Apostle Paul advises,

Let this mind be in you, which was also in Christ Jesus; who, being in the form of God, thought it not robbery to be equal to God but made Himself of no reputation and took upon Him the form of a servant and was made in the likeness of men. And being found in fashion as a man, He humbled Himself, and became obedient unto death, even the death of the cross ~ Philippians 2:5-8

When we begin to develop our minds through a spirit of humility, a spirit of obedience, a spirit of servitude, and a spirit of lowliness, we begin to experience the development of the seed which God has endowed us with. The natural mind operates in the spirit of "survival of the fittest," the spirit of presumption, and the spirit of disobedience. However, the Master taught: "Blessed are the poor in spirit; for theirs is the kingdom of heaven" (Matthew 5:3, KJV). The New Living Translation of the same verse says, "God blesses those who realize their need for Him." Indeed, it is at the point when we realize that we need God that God begins to develop the seed in us – and true holiness and purity take root in our hearts.

Victory begins with the name of Jesus on our lips; but it is not consummated until the nature of Jesus is in our hearts – Francis Frangipane

Notice that Frangipane said hearts and not mind? The true victory in our lives begins when the mind of Christ is not just on our lips but also in our hearts, "for with the heart man believeth unto righteousness; and with the mouth confession is made unto salvation" (Romans 10:10). In ancient Israel, the heart was not the seat of emotions, but rather the center of the will and rationality. If we are renewing our minds, we are *believing* that which God has planned for us and not just agreeing with it.

But they that wait upon the Lord shall renew their strength; they shall mount up with wings as eagles; they shall run, and not be weary, they shall walk and not faint. – Isaiah 40:31

The concept of renewal continues as seen in the prophetic and wise words of the prophet Isaiah. They provide us with a basis for waiting on the Lord. But what does it mean to wait on the Lord? To *wait on* means *to serve or act as a servant.* This clearly defines our purpose and the prerequisite for success and prosperity: if we wish to mount up with wings as eagles and soar to our success and prosperity, we have to wait on God. Jesus told His disciples that whoever wants to be the greatest must serve others since even He, in His infinite greatness, did not come to earth to be ministered unto, but to minister unto others. Therefore, to be successful and reach your full potential, you must serve.

In your quest for the things of God, you must be careful to "neglect not the gift that was given thee" (I Timothy 4:14). Each of us is born with the ability and gift to love God and to minister to Him – that is the way we were made! All He wants is for us to wait on

Him and give Him first place in our lives, and then we shall rise with wings as eagles and be strong. He said, "I am Alpha and Omega, the beginning and the end, the first and the last" (Revelation 22:13). We must, therefore, accord God due benevolence.

And be renewed in the spirit of your mind; and that ye put on the new man, which after God is created in righteousness and true holiness ~ Ephesians 4:23-24

Renewing one's mind is not only liberating, but it also ushers in newness in one's life. The spirit of poverty, both spiritual and physical, is something that can quite easily be conquered if only one can renovate the way one thinks. The reason that many church folks sit along the spiritual sidewalks begging for spiritual and physical bread is because they have not been educated and instructed about how to develop the seed God has planted in them. We will look into this closely later in the book, but it is imperative to realize that when you think you can, you can; when you think you cannot, surely you cannot.

If you want to change your life, you've got to do it immediately and flamboyantly ~ William James

Christians in the United States often get glimpses into the poverty and hunger that stalks the nations of Africa, South America, and other developing areas, thanks to the "omnipresent" media. These images rend our hearts and awaken great humanitarian desires within us, desires to alleviate the pain and suffering in the lives of those people – oh, especially the children. Being from Africa myself, I have seen a lot of people's lives changed simply by *an opportunity*. The Christian community in the United States lives at a time and in a place in which poverty as we imagine it is ridiculous to those that live in truly impoverished areas. What the dilemma seems to be is that God had made the *provision*, but the people have not caught the *vision*. As earlier stated, the endowment is the first thing that God gives to humanity and yet we are unable to capitalize on that endowment. I shudder to think of what might happen if God were to sever us from the vine!

The prophet Habakkuk questioned how Yahweh could use an evil nation like Babylonia to punish His own righteous people, Israel. Unfortunately today we are seeing the evil nation of Satan rise above us in both stature and spirit. However, like He told Israel, God is instructing us to "write the vision, and make it plain upon the tables, that he may run that readeth it. For the vision is yet for an appointed time, but at the end it shall speak, and not lie. Though it tarry, wait for it, because it will surely come, it will not tarry" (Habakkuk 2:2-3). I believe the appointed time has indeed come, and the Church must now get up and claim that which is rightfully hers!

We must be the change we wish to see in the world –Gandhi

Mahatma Gandhi once said "we should be the change we wish to see in the world." If we are to execute righteous change and authority, let us "do it immediately and flamboyantly." None of us knows the time or the hour in which the Son of Man shall return. Therefore, to avoid being caught naked and ashamed, let us begin to elevate our minds daily by "casting down imaginations, and every high thing that exalteth itself against the knowledge of God, and bring into captivity every thought to the obedience of Christ" (2 Corinthians 10:5).

It is absolutely incredible to watch the effects of a closed mind. I have met well-educated men and women whose minds are so tightly shut that a needle can hardly go through. By shutting their minds, they feel that they are keeping the bad elements out and indeed they may be. However, when you shut others out, you are also shutting yourself in. Jericho is a typical example.

Now Jericho was straightly shut up because of the children of Israel: none went out, and none came in – Joshua 6:1

Too often we think we are doing ourselves a great service by keeping out those elements that have caused us grief in the past, but in the process of doing so, we shut ourselves in and become prisoners – none come in and none go out.

Jericho is the first thing every man or woman who is seeking success must face. In order to get to Jerusalem, which is beyond the Jordan valley, you must go through Jericho, a walled and fortified city that lies directly in the heart of the valley. Jericho is the mind. Before any great feat is accomplished, we must conquer Jericho by tearing down the walls and burning it to the ground as Joshua and the children of Israel did.

The children of Israel, after forty years of wilderness wondering, were finally ready to enter the Promised Land, but standing in their way was Jericho. Every other army before them had been intimidated by the high walls and turned back because they could not conquer the fortifications. This time, however, the Lord told Joshua, "See, I have given into thine hand Jericho, and the king thereof, and the mighty men of valor." Joshua and Israel were therefore in a unique position to do something that nations had failed to do for years. Many of us have been told the same thing that the Lord told Joshua, but because we do not understand this concept, we turn back at the walls. This goes back to our premise that the Lord has already given us everything we need to be fruitful, multiply, replenish the earth, subdue it and have dominion. The Lord said to Hosea, "My people are destroyed for lack of knowledge." Many of God's people are being destroyed today because they lack knowledge.

We utilize the earth's natural resources by using them up, but we waste man's natural resources by not using them at all. This is the greatest tragedy of our time. Limitless potential is never realized: brilliant and talented singers are operating machinery all of their days; gifted doctors settle for telemarketing jobs – and they wonder what their destiny is! This unrealized potential does not only affect them, it invariably affects generation after generation. Moses tells us in Exodus 34:7 that the Lord visits the iniquity of fathers upon the children, and upon the children's children, unto the third and the fourth generation. Parents realize too late what they could have done in their own lives and so push their dreams and former abilities onto their children, such that their children end up being something that they were not intended to be.

I know for a fact that I am not a medical doctor and I have no talent for such a field. My abilities lie in speaking, teaching, writing and athletics. I believe it is absolutely sinful for me to try to be a medical doctor when that is not my talent. It is my firm stance that every human being is born with a measure of ability and what he does with it is more important than what he doesn't do with it. It is all in the mind. The Master once told of three servants:

> For the kingdom of Heaven is as a man traveling into a far country, who called his own servants and delivered unto them his goods. And unto one he gave five talents, to another two, and to another one, to every man according to his several ability; and straightway took his journey. Then he that had received the five talents went and traded with the same, and made them other five talents. And likewise he that had received two, he also gained other two. But he that had received one went and digged in the earth and hid his lord's money – Matthew 25:14-18

It is my understanding that talent and ability are two separate entities. Webster's dictionary defines ability as "powers of the mind[4]" or "mental gifts or endowments[5]." On the other hand, a Hebrew talent is an ancient weight and denomination of money. As mentioned earlier, we have already been given the ability to succeed. It follows, then, that the blessing is the ability; and the talents is the denomination or endowment of power given to us. Our being formed in the likeness of God gives us the innate ability to do great things while the talent is given to us according to our ability. Two of the servants multiplied the talents while one dug a hole and hid his lord's talent. Is this unlike what we do? We long for the seemingly attractive riches and wealth that talent, ability and hard work bring but hide our talent and expect it to somehow sprout out of the ground.

The Hebrew talent weighed 93 ¾ pounds[6]. The first servant had to work with 468 ¾ pounds while the servant with two talents worked with 187 ½ pounds. These two had heavier talents than had the one with one talent – his only weighed 93 ¾ pounds. However, to

21

him it was more profitable to hide the talent until his lord came back because he could not go beyond the scope of his mind to multiply what had been given to him.

Many of us have been given a talent or two, but our minds have been straightly shut up such that we have become paralyzed and rendered impotent. All the while, the ability or endowment and accompanying talents are waiting to be appropriated in our lives. It is not until we know what our mind is and has that we can properly appropriate the talents and ability God has blessed us with. Four important things you must always note about your mind are:

♦The mind is a *garden* that can be cultivated to potentially produce the harvest that we desire.

♦The mind is a *workshop* where the important decisions of life and eternity are molded and made.

♦The mind is an *armory* where the weapons for our victory or our destruction are forged

♦The mind is a *battlefield* where ALL the decisive battles of life are won or lost[7].

Until you decide to tear down the walls of your mind and become a person of excellence, you will wear yourself out wishing and hoping you could do, have and be what others do, have and are.

> *The world is endless, the universe inexhaustible, and the human brain will never be threatened with unemployment*
> *~ Genrich Altshuller, The Innovation Algorithm*

How right Altshuller was! As mentioned earlier, the brain is the container of the mind. There are a vast number of people that have given their brains and mind a vacation because not thinking for themselves is easier than thinking for themselves. The reason many folks are more comfortable in Egypt – in bondage – is because someone tells them when to get up, when to go to sleep, what to wear and what to eat. This clearly removes any manner of responsibility from the individual and places it on the master. You may have heard the aphorism, "You can take the man out of the ghetto but you can't take the ghetto out of the man." Many folks have been removed from the ghetto but the ghetto is still in them so they cannot grow and mature into the unique and empowered men and women they are supposed to be.

In her critically acclaimed book "A is for Attitude," Patricia Russell-McCloud says,

> Your brain is a complex and sensitive instrument, finely wired with divine circuitry that enables you to find and express meaning, deal with pleasure and pain, calmly cope with both emergencies or the routine, and fully sense all that surrounds you.

Your brain has been finely wired with divine circuitry and it is up to you to use that unique and divine circuitry, and to make the most out of it!

I was in St. Lucia, West Indies a few years ago and observed that most of the young men and women on the island had given up all hope of ever being or doing anything significant in their lives. Walking down their streets I was reminded of the young men and women of my home country, Zambia – they, too, have given up all hope of being or doing anything significant in and with their lives. I was speaking to several groups of middle school-aged boys and girls, and was touched to see that all they wanted was a chance. One of the young ladies, whom I affectionately nicknamed "my doctor," has plans to be a doctor; all she needs and seeks is the opportunity to do so. Meanwhile, here in the United States, relatively affluent young men and women are failing to make use of their minds in college and high school.

If you are one of those people that have been majoring in the minor, sitting on the bench while everyone else is playing, and thinking that you could never amount to anything because you're just not smart enough, it is time to change the color of your thoughts. You must think more positively about yourself and your circumstances; use them to better yourself. In utilizing and appropriating your brain power, you will open up a wave of potential such that you will not have time in your day to think thoughts of doom and destruction.

It is when we change the color of our thoughts and our vocabulary that we become something we have never been before. You see, you don't pay the price for good health; you enjoy the benefits of good health. You do not pay the price for a good marriage; you pay the price for a poor one. You enjoy the benefits of a good one. You do not pay the price for success; you pay the price for failure.

James Allen, in his critically acclaimed book, *As a Man Thinketh*, meditated on the Biblical principal "for as he thinketh in his heart, so is he," saying,

> A man's mind may be likened to a garden, which may be intelligently cultivated or allowed to run wild; but whether cultivated or neglected, it must and will, bring forth. If no useful seeds are put into it, then an abundance of useless weed-seeds will fall therein, and will continue to produce their kind.

Indeed, some people have exceptional cognitive abilities but the average IQ is 100 with a standard deviation of 15. We all, therefore, have the ability to utilize our brains and minds, cultivate in them the seeds we require for growth and success, and reap the benefits of a utilized garden whether we know it or not.

The subconscious mind is the source of all inspiration, all motivation, and the excitement that rushes over you when aroused by a new idea or possibility

In today's fast paced world, employers are looking for cognitively competent men and women to help them run their businesses. It does not take too much cognitive effort to flip burgers and say, "Welcome to McDonalds, may I take your order?" But it certainly takes a lot more cognitive thought and effort to figure out ways in which profits can be maximized as the general manager. "People with fast, flexible minds are best poised to succeed in the twenty-first century," says Patricia Russell-McCloud – and right she is. Today's fast-paced world of the Internet, E-Commerce and the mobile phone requires men and women that are "on top of things." It comes as no surprise, then, that the Lord is also looking for men and women that have flexible minds and brains that are constantly working to run His business. Clearly, those with the wilderness attitude, poverty spirit and slave mentality have no place in the good life that a mind and brain working at full potential affords.

Frederick Douglas once stated: *Strive to add to your knowledge. Don't get bitter; get better.* If we begin to realize that we have been endowed with something by God that must be used, we are closer to reaching our potential. I saw it once written that the brain is a priceless resource that is given to each of us free at birth. Each of us has the priceless resource of the brain and now it is up to us to begin to develop it and nurture it to produce the desired fruits.

Death and life are in the power of the tongue; and they that love it shall eat thereof – Proverbs 18:21

We have so far established that in order to effect change in our minds we need to change the color of our thoughts. How do you change the color of your thoughts? *With words.* Think about it: what makes you think you can't do it? *Words.* What makes you afraid to do the extraordinary? *Words.* Life and death *are* in the power of the tongue! You have abounding power in your tongue and mouth; and in that power lies life and death. Which one you choose to appropriate in your life is your choice. *One kind word can warm three winters* says a Japanese proverb. There is weight and power in your words.

Thou art snared by the words of thy mouth; thou art taken with the words of thy mouth – Proverbs 6:2

Every man is responsible for his own words. Some people cannot keep a secret even if their life depends on it! The reason many folks are living in poverty and lack today is because they have snared themselves with words of poverty and lack. They think like they're poor and they speak like they're poor. It, therefore, comes as no surprise that they *are* poor. When you say something long enough, you are bound to become what you say.

In his book, *Self-talk*, psychologist Dr. David Stoops gives us interesting insight about the words spoken in the walls of our hearts and minds:

We usually speak out loud at the rate of 150 to 200 words per minute. Some research suggests that we talk privately to ourselves in our thoughts at the rate of approximately 1300 words per minute. Since many of our thoughts take the form of mental images or concepts, we can think of something in a fleeting moment that would take us many minutes of verbal speech to describe.

Considering what Dr. Stoop says, we see how easy it is to ensnare ourselves by foolish and negative talk. Much has been said and written about the words that actually *do* come out of our lips but I believe there is more damage being done by the words that are conjured up and said in the walls of our minds.

"Mend your speech a little, lest it may mar your fortunes," wrote William Shakespeare in *King Lear*. How many fortunes have been marred by ill-timed and ill-thought words? How many people have been deterred from their pursuits because of ill-thought words that broke their spirit and their drive? You see, unlike the old west, being quick on the draw [with your tongue] leads you to death. Frederick Douglas, in his book "Narrative of the life of Frederick Douglas: An American Slave" wrote, "A still tongue makes a wise head. The way in which you use your tongue, lips and mouth invariably shows your intellect and potential for success."

Tis' the mind that makes the body rich – Shakespeare

The power of words is far beyond what we can imagine. Dr. Paul Yonggi Cho, pastor of the world's largest church in Seoul, Korea, writes brilliantly on the matter:

If someone keeps on saying, "I'm going to become weak," then right away, all the nerves receive that message, and say, "Let's prepare to become weak, for we've received instructions from our control communication that we should become weak." And they adjust their physical attitudes to weakness. If someone says, "I have no ability, I can't do this job," then right away all the nerves begin to declare the same things and prepare themselves to be part of an incapable person.

He continues by adding,

> What you speak, you are going to get. If you keep on saying that you are poor, then all of your system conditions tend to attract poverty, and you will be at home in poverty; you would rather be poor. Before you can be changed, you must change your language. If you do not change your language, you cannot change yourself.

Coming from the man running the world's largest church, I do not need anymore convincing. I have no doubt that the naysayers did not envision the vision he had to run the world's largest church. I know, for a fact, that the color of his thinking was not dull and dejected – it was bright and colorful!

Ralph Waldo Emerson once wrote that "a man becomes what he thinks about most of the time" and that "the key to every man is his thought." Our thoughts and words are very, very indicative of what we are capable of doing – even with the abundant potential we may have. "The only thing any person has complete, unchallenged control over is his thought – his state of mind," says Napoleon Hill. You and I have the unique capacity of thought and speech so what is contained in both of these is very, very important.

I will never forget the words of Tom Robbins in his book *Jitterbug Perfume*. He wrote: "To achieve the marvelous, it is precisely the unthinkable that must be thought." Too many people are living below their potential because they think like everyone else and want to be like everyone else – underpaid, undervalued, underprivileged, undermined, underdeveloped, and undersold!

Everything becomes a little different as soon as it is spoken out aloud – Hermann Hesse

> A son and his father are walking in the mountains when suddenly, his son falls, hurts himself and screams, "AAA-hhhhhhh!!!"
> To his surprise, he hears the voice repeating, somewhere in the mountain, "AAA-hhhhhhh!!!"
> Curious, he yells, "Who are you?"
> He receives the answer, "Who are you?"
> Angered at the response, he screams, "Coward!"
> He receives the answer, "Coward!"
> He looks at his father and asks, "What's going on?"
> The father smiles and says, "My son, pay attention."
> And then he screams to the mountain, "I admire you!"
> The voice answers, "I admire you!"
> Again the man screams, "You are a champion!"
> The voice answers, "You are a champion!"
> The boy is surprised, but does not understand.
> Then the father explains, "People call this ECHO, but really this is LIFE[8]."

You will get out of life exactly what you throw at it. Irrespective of the time it takes to get your harvest, you will definitely reap what you sow. Phrases like "I admire you" and "You are a champion" allow you to view life with the uplook you ought to have.

You are snared by the words of *your* mouth, not the words of another man or woman's mouth. No matter what people say to you or about you, you are not bound by their words – you are bound by your *own* words. Negativity, discouragement and disappointment are part of the high-achievers day. It becomes fatal when negativity, discouragement and disappointed come from the high-achiever's *own* mouth.

Words are the only things that last forever

William Hazlitt, in his book *Table-Talk: On Thought and Action*, writes, "Words are the only things that last forever." Just as a kind word can warm up three winters, a negative word can have resounding effects on you if you say it long enough. I have no doubt that every time that young boy spoke from that moment on, he spoke uplifting and positive words. Try it...

Chapter Three

Attitude is everything; altitude is determined by attitude. High achievers shoot for the stars; if they fall short of their mark, at least they come back with stardust in their hands

An elderly carpenter, ready to retire, told his employer-contractor of his plans to leave the house-building business, and live a more leisurely life with his wife. He would miss the paycheck, but he needed to retire, and they could get by. The contractor was sorry to see his good worker go, and asked if he would build just one more house as a personal favor. The carpenter said yes, but in time it was easy to see that his heart was not in his work. He resorted to shoddy workmanship, and used inferior materials. It was an unfortunate way to end a dedicated career. When the carpenter finished his work, the employer came to inspect the house. He handed the front-door key to the carpenter and said, "This is your house. My gift to you." The carpenter was shocked! What a shame! If he had only known he was building his own house, he would have done it all so differently.

So it is with us. We build our lives, a day at a time, often putting less than our best into the building. Then with a shock we realize we have to live in the house we have built. If we could do it over, we'd do it differently. But we cannot go back.

You are the carpenter. Each day you hammer a nail, place a board, or erect a wall. "Life is a do-it-yourself project," someone once said. Your attitudes and the choices you make today build the "house" you live in tomorrow. Build wisely[1]!

The December 1993 issue of *Hartline Newsletter* printed an article citing what would happen if 99.9% were good enough. The following is a list of their findings:

1. 2,000,000 documents will be lost by the IRS this year
2. 22,000 checks will be deducted from wrong bank accounts in the next 60 minutes
3. 1,314 telephone calls will be misplaced by telecommunications services every minute

31

4. 12 babies will be given to the wrong parents each day
5. 2,488 books will be shipped with the wrong cover on them
6. Over 5.5 million cases of soft drinks will be produced in the next 12 months that will be flatter than a bad tire
7. 20,000 incorrect drug prescriptions will be written in the next 12 months…

…All if 99.9% is good enough!

I know a lot of us would be happy with the first one! However, many of us are working under par because of several reasons ranging from "because I am paid less for the hard work I do" to "it's not important." Like the carpenter, it is not for someone else that we are building the house – it is our own house we are building with inferior materials and an inferior attitude. 99.9% is *not* good enough in any area of life. Would you be happy with 99.9% of your paycheck? 99.9% of your spouse? 99.9% of your child? Not many people would be happy with 99.9% of anything – that should include your potential!

Attitude can either make or break a relationship, an organization or an individual. Attitude constitutes one's disposition and one's condition of mind, body and soul. The attitude one presents himself with to others or to oneself ultimately determines the distance that he will travel in his plans – it will depend *entirely* upon his attitude. Some people want to be C.E.O., Chairman of the Board, or President of a company while others are desperate to accomplish such goals and expend all their energies towards these goals. They are desperate to attain a particular end such that all they are consumed with are the means and ways to attain those ends.

Attitude encompasses almost ninety percent of our lives; it is the way we act or react to the situations, trials and tests that being alive affords us. Each of us has dreams and pursuing those dreams should be the most exciting part of our lives. Percy Sutton, lawyer, politician and successful entrepreneur, concerning pursuing the dream, once said, "It means daring to reach, to climb, to crawl, to scratch, to get back up when you've been knocked down, to push forward – ever forward – to forgive. It means sacrificing everything, if necessary, to carve out a place for your own existence. It means living." If we are to reach out and attain that excellence that our Creator intended for us, we have to be hungry enough to reach, climb, crawl, scratch, get back up when we're pushed and refuse to give in!

And he said, "Let me go, for the day breaketh." And he said, "I will not let thee go, except thou bless me." – Genesis 32:26

A very interesting character in the Bible was desperate and hungry for something he was pursuing. Because of his hunger, a nation was born; but more immediate, he got what he hungered, scratched and scraped for – a blessing. Jacob, the son of Isaac, was really obsessed (for lack of a better term) about the blessing of God. Like many men and women, he was already endowed with the blessing to be fruitful, multiply, replenish, subdue, and have dominion. However, like all hungry people, he knew that was not all. There had to be more!

Jacob, whose name means "heel-grabber" or "trickster," slyly stole the blessing from his twin brother, Esau, and wrestled with "a man" until the break of day in order to secure a blessing (Genesis 27-35). The irony of this story is that Jacob, always the schemer, was already preordained to prevail against "the man" he wrestled with. However, God will not just give humanity additional blessings and endowments without man having to play a part. The Master taught: "Blessed are they that do hunger and thirst after righteousness; for they shall be filled" (Matthew 5:6). In other words, empowered are those that are hungry to know, experience, and understand the ways of God!

It must be understood that the empowerment to be fruitful, multiply, replenish, subdue and have dominion over the earth is something that the Lord has already given to us. However, this is not the end of the Lord's blessings. It is only the beginning! For one to attain the multitude of blessings God has in store for us, we must be hungry, seeking that which He is trying to give us.

To accomplish this, one must have the right attitude and disposition about the feat in question and the One that gave us the feat in the first place. Though we think *we* have conjured up the plans and desires to be successful, we have not. The Father has given us those desires because that is *His* nature – He is successful and lacking nothing! Therefore, all we are doing is following in the ways and patterns of Him with whom we have to do.

We must position ourselves in a way that will be conducive for God to operate. This is so that we may attain the right attitude and disposition. Nothing that needs to be done in us and on this earth can be done without *our* permission. In other words, in Genesis 1:28, God gave us dominion or supreme authority to rule on this earth. Can you begin to operate in a king's domain without first seeking permission? Absolutely not! When Adam and Eve sinned, they handed the keys of the world over to Satan, but when Jesus died on the cross, He took the keys and gave them back to us. Therefore, God needs *our* cooperation if He is to accomplish His goal in us, and in the world around us. *Cooperation* positions us to have the right attitude and disposition to accomplish the impossible, to dream the undreamable, think the unthinkable, do the improbable, and to be all that God would have us be.

The hammer shatters glass but also forges steel – Russian Proverb

A Russian proverb says: "The hammer shatters glass but also forges steel." Our disposition and attitude determines whether we will be shattered like glass or forged like steel. Remember, however, for steel to be forged by a hammer, the steel must first endure the test of fire. Many people shatter at the first sign of trouble or when it seems that God is "absent" or "uncaring." The *key* to being forged and molded is that one must first stand the test of fire; "microwave achievers" are people who would like to be forged and molded by God but they are not willing to first be tested and tried by fire. They are willing to sit on the throne but not work to get there; often they do not even show a glimpse of hunger for it.

Don't let anyone ever set your limitations. Know what your dreams will cost and be willing to pay the price
– Bill Pinckney

Bill Pinckney, the first African-American to ever sail around the world, advised that to attain one's goals, one must know what they will cost and be willing to pay the price for them. This, my friend, is where many a man or woman stops because "it's too hard" or because "I can't do it." With the hunger to achieve must come the assuredness that you *can* do it. The 14th century poet, Ralph Waldo Emerson, once said: "The world makes way for the person who knows where he or she is going." Too many people do not know where they are going; hence, neither they nor God can pave a way for them in life. Frederick Douglas, in his autobiography "Narrative of the life of Frederick Douglas: An American slave," wrote:

> "That which to him was a great evil, to be carefully shunned, was to me a great good, to be diligently sought; and the argument which he so warmly urged against my learning to read, only served to inspire me with a desire and determination to."

Frederick Douglas was determined to learn how to read, and the more his master afflicted him or tried to dissuade him, the hungrier and more determined and diligent he became. That is the exact attitude you must have about attaining your goals and dreams.

It is very easy to see the difficulties in a situation, and you will often encounter those that are very capable faultfinders but completely lack the ability to solve the problems that they so eagerly uncover. Thomas Fuller, in his book *Gnomologia*, wrote: "All things are difficult before they are easy." William Ellery Channing also said, "Difficulties are meant to rouse, not discourage." Anything that is being purified will go through a time of testing in fire. Before that gold or platinum wedding band you've seen in the mall became that expensive and much desired ornament, it had to be purified and tested in fire. Before that diamond on that wedding or engagement ring became that painfully expensive solitaire, it had to go through stringent trying and testing in fire. What, therefore, is so odd about you being tried and tested in the fires of life?

The only way hunger can be rectified is by filling one's belly with food. The only way to fulfill one's hunger for success is to attain the blessing of God. The only way to attain the blessing of God is to seek Him by relating to Him. The only way to relate to and with Him is to acknowledge Him. Proverbs 3:5-6 says: "Trust in the Lord with all thine heart and lean not unto thine own understanding. In all thy ways acknowledge Him and He shall direct thy paths." This world is a very tricky and difficult place but with the assistance and guidance of God, nothing is impossible.

But God hath chosen the foolish things of the world to confound the wise; and God hath chosen the weak things of the world to confound the things which are mighty; and the base things of the world, and things which are despised, hath God chosen, yea, and things which are not, to bring to nought things that are; that no flesh shall glory in His presence
~ 1 Corinthians 1:27-29

I heard it once stated that throughout recorded history, when it comes to the subject of achievement and progress, this one idea holds true: *The crowd is always wrong!* Once again, the traditions of man make the Word of God ineffective because to the human mind, if everyone is doing something or thinking alike, then it is right. "To follow foolish precedents, and wink with both our eyes, is easier than to think," says William Cowper in his book *Tirocinium.*

November 18, 1978, marked one of the most horrifying religious tragedies of modern times.

The Reverend Jim Jones, the founder of Jonestown, and his church, the People's Temple, moved to Redwood Valley, California. Jones was a social activist who had pushed hard for racial integration. However, his teachings deviated from mainstream Christianity; he even claimed to be a living god and claimed to have raised forty-three people from the dead. In 1977, under increasing pressure and criticism from both secular and religious organizations, he and many of his congregation moved to Guyana and carved the Jonestown community out of the wild, dense jungle. However, criticism and pressure continued, especially from disaffected members, until the Jonestown leadership chose mass suicide as the way out, the prelude to a happy reunion on "the other side." Nine hundred and fourteen human beings including women and children died after consuming Kool Aid laced with cyanide in this collective religious ritual of "revolutionary suicide[2]."

My first question when I read about this was: What was everyone thinking?! The crowd isn't always right; did those nine hundred and fourteen people know that? Today's world is governed by trends and fads, and each of these tend to cloud our better judgment because conformity seems to be one of man's most fundamental goals. However, people that are hungry for success are unaffected by trends or the crowd. I can say for a fact that when I decided to move to the United States, my friends and family were less than enthusiastic about my decision, to say the least. Why? Because a nineteen-year-old young man is not supposed to just leave home, and all its entanglements in order to move across the globe to a land he has never visited or seen. Well, I moved anyway, and several years have now passed in which I have truly excelled only because this was a hunger that had to be filled or I would have lost my mind.

An "anonymous" writer once wrote that "what happens *to* a man is less significant than what happens *within* him" (emphasis mine). Indeed, the battle in any man's life begins within himself. Only you know the inner man or woman in you and you must confront him or her and find a way in which to work together towards the goal before you. My "surrogate" father, George Eberly, always tells me: "Boy, you've got the world by its tail. You can do anything you wanna do!" Most of us have the world by its tail and if we would only hold on long enough, as the cowboy works to stay on that bull for eight seconds, we will achieve each goal before us in style.

No paper contribution will ever give us self-government. No amount of speeches will ever make us fit for self-government. It is only our conduct that will fit us for it
– Gandhi during a speech in 1916

Mohandas "Mahatma" Gandhi hit the nail on the head when he said that it is *only our conduct* that gives us self-government. To relate this to ourselves, we need to think about the things that allow us to be who we are. How can you tell the difference between salt and sugar? Salt is sour, sugar is sweet. That sweetness or sourness is the flavor with which we associate sugar or salt. In the same way, both God and man will associate us with our attitude every time we are saying something or doing something.

THE REBECCA PRINCIPLE[3]

And the servant ran to meet her, and said, "Let me, I pray thee, drink a little water of thy pitcher." And she said, "Drink my lord." And she hasted, and let down her pitcher upon her hand, and gave him to drink. And when she was done giving him drink, she said, "I will draw water for thy camels also, until they have done drinking." And she hasted, and emptied her pitcher into the trough, and ran again unto the well to draw water, and drew for all his camels – Genesis 24:17-20

The memory of the days in which we woke up very early in the morning to draw water from the well on our farm in Zambia is still fresh in my mind. We would fill two-hundred-liter drums with water in order to water mum's roses. This process took at least an hour and a half for three men and two young boys to complete. We used large containers, rather than pitchers, to draw enough water to fill the drums. The most agonizing part of this chore was pushing the drums uphill towards the roses – now you know why I was so eager to move to America!

It is for this reason that I can identify with Rebecca. Somewhere around her mid to late teens, she was on her usual errand of drawing water at the well when Abraham's servant and his ten camels rode into town. Genesis chapter 24 tells the story of how Abraham sent his servant to Nahor to fetch Isaac a wife. The servant took with him ten camels and some gifts, and prayed that God would show him who the lucky lady would be. He prayed that the damsel would give him water to drink and also give water to his camels – and sure enough, that's what Rebecca did. I know you're thinking, "Yeah, so what?" Well, let us examine the story a little more closely.

First, the pitcher she was using is what is called in Hebrew a *kad¹*. A *kad* was an earthen or metallic vessel used for domestic purposes and could carry, perhaps five liters of water. Now, Abraham's servant had ten camels that had traveled from Canaan to Mesopotamia. This is not a simple journey; Canaan was near the Mediterranean Sea while Mesopotamia was near the Persian Gulf. These camels were utterly tired and thirsty by the end of this journey. Although a camel can travel nine days without water, when it does get to "refuel", it drinks between 100 and 120 liters of water at a time. Therefore, ten camels would require a minimum of a thousand liters of water at the end of such a journey. Rebecca would therefore need to run back and forth from the well 200 times! Rather than shrinking from the daunting task, however, she "hasted, and emptied her pitcher into the trough, and ran again unto the well to draw water, and drew for all his camels." She *ran*!

Strive earnestly to add to your knowledge. Don't get bitter, get better – Frederick Douglas

This endeavor that Rebecca engaged herself in was indeed an inconvenience. However, she decided to get better rather than bitter. Each situation that we face has the potential of doing one of two things: enriching our lives in some way, or becoming a stumbling block that trips us up. In Rebecca's case, this single act of kindness allowed Rebecca to be the great, great, great, great, great, great, great, great, great grandmother of the Messiah. If we can only strive to see the larger picture, rather than the miniscule one that we are starring in, we will begin to achieve greatness.

The Rebecca Principle is simply utilizing every day and opportunity life affords us to grow spiritually and to add to our knowledge of God, others and ourselves.

If you're looking at the sun, you seldom see any shadows
– Helen Keller

Attitude will always dictate the heights to which you rise. If you have a shabby, shallow, narrow attitude, your outlook on and performance in life will also be shabby, shallow and narrow. Some people's attitudes lead them to be obtuse and miss the essence of their being. Many Christians seem content to just wait for heaven, and fail to realize that life on earth is meant to be enjoyed and utilized as a training ground for the good life to come.

Patricia Russell-McCloud wrote, "Your attitude is one of your greatest assets. It is your attitude and your thoughts that will determine whether you master all that is available to you from life's rich platter." Too many folks are living life under par because they have terrible attitudes towards themselves and life. With a good attitude, however, we always come out of situations stronger, bigger and better. As Zig Ziglar put it, "when the outlook isn't good, and it often isn't, try the up look – it's always good."

I was in Moscow, Russia several years ago and noticed that the attitude among people in the city was terribly poor. The women hardly ever smiled and the men treated outsiders as if they had somehow caused the misery surrounding them. What these poor souls did not realize is that a good attitude is like a ray of sunlight in winter – it changes everything. Life is often unfair and unpleasant, but the manner in which we react to circumstances and the attitude with which we face these difficulties can make a world of difference.

Nelson Mandela, former political prisoner and president of the Republic of South Africa is a true testimony to the power of a good attitude. After being locked in prison for twenty-six years, he emerged to lead South Africa out of apartheid and into democracy. What a brilliant attitude Mandela displayed when he was shown embracing F.W. de Klerk, the former South African president who had incarcerated him for twenty-six years of his life. This is definitely an image that reflects both constancy to purpose and the power of a positive attitude.

40

"Attitude is beyond mindset, for it encompasses your thoughts and your actions. It determines how you respond to your environment, and why you say and do the things you do. It is an indication of your sensitivity on an issue or your blatant disregard. Simply put, attitude is your choice," writes Patricia Russell-McCloud. In our world of "if it works for you, do it" and countless incidences of situational ethics, attitude certainly is a choice. We choose to say what we say and do what we do — whether good or bad.

Keep thy heart with all diligence; for out of it are the issues of life – Proverbs 4:23

It follows, then, that if our attitude determines our altitude, we must be exceedingly careful to guard our minds and our hearts. As stated in Proverbs chapter four, the issues of life flow out of the heart, and if we allow the filth of the world and the raw attitudes it promotes to enter into our innermost being we will hardly accomplish anything meaningful in our lives. Attitude is a choice that we make to do the right things at the right time and in the right way.

When I first began playing basketball with my older brothers and their friends, they constantly put me down. I was too short and wasn't strong enough to be playing with them but I kept at it. A few years later, I was one of the youngest players in the Zambia Basketball Association Premier League and was leading my high school squad in rebounds, points, steals and assists! Shortly thereafter, I was named to the Zambia National Basketball Team and ranked among the top five players in the nation. I could not have accomplished this feat had I not had the right attitude and kept my heart with all diligence. When most of the other players in the league went out drinking after the game, I would review the mistakes I had made and plan how to rectify them the next time. When the time came for a national team to be selected, there was no question as to whether or not I would be picked. Most of what we have in life is because of conscious choices that we make. The young woman that decides to toy with premarital sex may find herself pregnant or infected with HIV; the star quarterback that decides to toy with alcohol finds himself in a car accident, his dreams of a great athletic career dashed to pieces. Choices...

Patricia Russell-McCloud continues to meditate upon attitude when she says:

Your thoughts direct what is and what will be, where you'll go and what you'll accomplish in life. You alone determine how far you can go in life, and the possibilities are endless. No family members, friends, foes, teachers, counselors, mentors, preachers, or employers, no one else can determine your plight or progress. YOU can exceed your potential. YOU can exceed every test, every evaluation, every expectation, every study, every database, every demographic compilation of statistical information on like individuals who, by all reports, based on scientific analysis, should not go beyond where they are.

It's all about YOU! You can either choose to let your family, friends, employers or circumstances determine how high you rise, or you can make the choice to take charge and reach your potential.

With every change in your life comes opposition. Folks that are used to seeing you on their level do their best to get you to stay right where you are. It's like crabs in a bucket – they keep pulling each other down! What you must remember, however, is that there is no traffic jam up in space.

Dr. Dennis Kimbro, in his book *What Makes the Great Great* says this about attitude:

Attitude outweighs education and comes before wealth. It's more important than circumstances, than heartbreak, than success, than what other people think, say, or do. It's more important than appearances, giftedness, or skill. Attitude will make or break an organization, a company, a school, a church, a home, a race, an enterprise, and yes, an individual.

With these words, Dr. Kimbro hit the nail on the head. The attitude that we bring to any situation is far more important that the outcome of that situation.

What happens to a man is less significant than what happens within him

A positive attitude has resounding effects on the quality of life...

Chapter Four

Character maketh a man –
Edna Gwen Makai

In my youth, my mother often seemed to me to be an unbearably wicked woman. She "ruthlessly" filtered my friends, never allowing me to associate with anyone who could possibly contaminate my life, or the dream of the future she envisioned for me.

Although she frequently embarrassed me, and often frustrated my siblings and I, she would always tell us that we were not like any other children and that she did everything she did because she loved us. I never quite understood what my mother meant until I became a man, and was able to look back over my upbringing and the values that my mother instilled in me. In essence, what my mother raised me to understand was that *character maketh a man.*

It is vital in our world today to understand that good character precedes our every move. A few years ago I had the opportunity to transfer to a State University from a community college at which I had been both attending and working. When the time came to make the move, my boss, who happened to be a former student and employee at the university to which I was transferring, called the university admissions office to secure a position for me.

When I attended the interview I was pleased to find out that my character had preceded me thanks to my former employer's phone call. The interviewers treated me as though they had known me for years. Needless to say, I got the job. Character, my friend, maketh a man!

Character is critical in order to realize the blessings and endowments God has placed in your lap. In this chapter, we will look at four young men that would neither bend nor compromise in character to accommodate an easier lifestyle.

> But Daniel purposed in his heart that he would not defile himself with the portion of the king's meat, nor with the wine which he drank. Therefore, he requested of the prince of the eunuchs that he might not defile himself. And the prince of the eunuchs said unto Daniel, "I fear my lord the king, who hath appointed your meat and your drink. For why should he see your faces worse looking than the children which are of your sort? Then shall ye make me endanger my head to the king." Then said Daniel to Melzar,

whom the prince of the eunuchs had set over Daniel, Hananiah, Mishael and Azariah, "Prove thy servants, I beseech thee, ten days and let them give us pulse to eat, and water to drink. Then let our countenances be looked upon before thee and the countenance of the children that eat of the portion of the king's meat; and as thou seest, deal with thy servants." So he consented to them in this matter, and proved them ten days. And at the end of ten days their countenances appeared fairer and fatter in flesh than all the children which did eat the portion of the king's meat — Daniel 1:8, 10-16

The Babylonians continually searched their empire for talented young men to be trained as wise courtiers for the imperial court[1]. When King Nebuchadnezzar conquered Jerusalem, he assigned a high officer of his court to pick out the best and brightest from the Jewish nobility[2] — "youths without blemish, handsome and skillful in all wisdom, endowed with knowledge, understanding, learning, and competent to serve in the king's palace" (Daniel 1:4).

Among those chosen were Daniel and three of his companions, Hananiah, Mishael, and Azariah. Their training was under the direction of Ashpenaz, the king's chief eunuch, who gave them each a Babylonian name. Daniel became Belteshazzar, and the others Shadrach, Meshach, and Abednego, respectively. These young men embarked on a three-year education that began with learning to speak Aramaic, and included all of the scientific and diplomatic skills that a courtier needed to work effectively in the rarefied atmosphere of the most powerful court of the day. Their privileged position entitled courtiers to a portion of the food prepared for the king himself — the best in the land — so that they would mature in health and strength worthy of their intended roles in the empire.

Daniel, however, immediately showed himself to be unwavering and disciplined in his allegiance to the traditions of his people, the Jews. Although he did not resist the call to serve as a courtier to the king, he insisted that "he would not defile himself with the portion of the king's meat, nor with the wine he drank" (Daniel 1:8). Instead, he asked to be given "pulse to eat, and water to drink" (Daniel 1:12).

The literal translation for the "pulse" they asked to be given is greens – veggies! After ten days, these Jewish boys that ate cabbage and drank water looked "fairer and fatter in the flesh" than those that ate lobster, steak and fries from the king's table! Eating from the king's table would have constituted a violation of the Jewish *kosher* laws[3], or dietary laws. Therefore, while the other young Jewish trainees in the king's court knocked themselves out with lobster, steak and fries, Daniel, Hananiah, Mishael and Azariah refused to compromise.

The opposite of compromise is character – Frederick Douglas

This attitude and outward display of character positioned Daniel for greatness such that the king made him "a great man, and gave him many great gifts, and made him ruler over the whole province of Babylon, and chief of the governors over all the wise men of Babylon" (Daniel 2:48), and at Daniel's request, the king "set Shadrach, Meshach, and Abednego over the affairs of the province of Babylon" (Daniel 2:49) Daniel's character was so strong that King Nebuchadnezzar inquired of him and his friends in all matters of wisdom and understanding. The Bible even says that their advice was found to be ten times better than all the magicians and astrologers in the king's realm! Character *maketh* a man!

He who steals my purse steals trash, but he who steals my good name, steals all – William Shakespeare

What do you think people remember most about those they come in contact with: what they look like, or what kind of people they are? As superficial as humans supposedly are, eight out of ten times people will not describe others by their physical characteristics, but rather by their personality, temperament or attitude. Think about some of the closest people to you. Do you look at them in terms of their physical attributes before you look at their character?

If there is one thing that never gets old, it is constancy and consistency in character. Can you imagine a man that is so temperamental and unpredictable that you don't know how to approach him? So it is with a man that cannot be consistent in his character: his reputation as a great businessman, athlete or pilot will always precede him. There is no better form of advertisement than word of mouth.

Recently I had lunch with two ministers and conversation turned to a man that had done a terrible job repairing one of the minister's cars. The man showed no indication of remorse, or intention to compensate the minister. This minister will undoubtedly not be referring anyone he knows to this particular mechanic, and the man's poor performance may have caused him to lose some customers. This man's lack of character and integrity now not only precedes him, but chases him as well.

HOW FAR WILL I GO?

Though success in life is potentially limitless, limitation lines must be drawn in the form of standards of conduct, both in business and in personal life. These standards should be uniquely and individually formulated. For instance, the behavior of children in the home must be set by parents. The conduct of parents as role models in the home and their professional conduct must also be a standard formulated. Such standards and limitations provide a sound basis for proper judgment in dealing with matters pertaining to one's life, and also provide direction in all endeavors that lie along the path to success.

Character is a reserve force, which acts directly by presence and without means – Ralph Waldo Emerson

There are people who wish to be successful at all costs, sometimes at the expense of their own family. However, a principled person whose family is at the top of his or her list of priorities would not make such a sacrifice. Integrity requires three steps: (1) *discerning* what is right and what is wrong; (2) *acting* on what you have discerned, even at personal cost; and (3) *saying openly* that you are acting on your understanding of right from wrong[4].

Our integrity is all we are left with at the end of the day, and at the end of our lives. Money cannot buy the priceless virtue of integrity.

Take drug dealers, for example: although they may become terribly wealthy, it is through dishonest means and they are never approved by those outside their world of crime and violence. All we truly have is our word, and integrity gives us credibility in our interaction with others. Stephen Covey, a best selling author and public speaker, wrote that integrity is "the foundation of trust, which is essential to cooperation and long-term personal and interpersonal growth." All we have is our word and we must, therefore, be wise in keeping it.

As a young boy, I was not able to be trusted around money, as I found it convenient to "use" it. In other words, I was a thief! But the effects of that regrettable habit, even after I repented, were far worse than the act of stealing itself. I lost my parents' respect and trust. And from then on out, every time something went missing...

Integrity is an integral part of success. It is a virtue that has to be cultivated and nurtured by the individual that is seeking not only to become successful but is seeking to remain successful. Keeping your word and being honest and trustworthy is the straightest, surest path to respect and success.

It is infinitely more precious to be nobly remembered than to be nobly born.

Think about the eulogy that will one day be read at your funeral! How do you want to be remembered? Think about these words: *It is infinitely more precious to be nobly remembered than to be nobly born.*

WHAT DO I STAND FOR?

My late father has been a major pillar of strength and wisdom in my development as a young man. Being a "military man," he drilled into me the discipline that is required in young men from my country. He often emphasized standing for what was right and never forgetting where I was from. I remember once spelling my last name as "Mcai" and not "Makai." He threw such a fit that I was upset with him for days. He asked me what it was about the family name that I was not pleased with and why I wanted to change my name. I didn't have much of an answer for him, it turned out, because there was no particular reason other than it was "cool" and I thought it looked more sophisticated.

In all honesty though, I was just trying to be someone and something that I was not.

The measure of a man's real character is what he would do if he would never be found out ~ Thomas Macaulay

It is very important to clearly ascertain what you stand for. Everyone has their opinion about how you must live your life but the most important opinion, besides that of God, is yours! I strongly believe that helping young men and young women to define what they stand for is but the beginning of the resolution of a number of social ailments, including teen pregnancies and drug abuse.

So many people in our society today are unable to carve in stone what they stand for and stand behind those values. This gives rise to many, as I term them, "passengers." You see, on every team, whether it's a basketball team or computer networking team, there are some that tend to just ride along on the team bus but play no active, unique role on the team. I don't know what kind of person you are, but I personally like to be upfront and significant in all my endeavors. Knowing what one stands for moves one from being a statistic, a wondering generality, to being significant.

I learned from my father that defining what I stood for gave rise to my confidence in who I was; it was a cushion for me whenever I fell, and it developed my character. An important part of setting standards and defining what one stands for is actually finding out where and what we come from. It is so sad to see how few Americans have researched their origins and family history; similarly, few Zambians have tried to remain close to their own culture, especially the language. This separation from our heritage has a two-fold effect on our society, even though we are moving towards a more "universal" and global culture: we lose our sense of dignity, and lose our unique flavor, our "American-ness" or "Zambian-ness". What good is salt if it loses its saltiness? Can you picture salt and pepper both moving towards being like sugar? It is exactly the same with our individual beliefs, opinions and priorities. No two humans on earth have the same fingerprints. This suggests that we are all unique. We may act alike and do similar things but no two people are the same, not even twins.

All of your scholarship, all of your study of Shakespeare and Wordsworth would be in vain if at the same time you did not build your character and attain mastery over your thoughts and your actions - Gandhi

Speaking to a college group, Mohandas "Mahatma" Gandhi spoke about the importance of combining the acquisition of intellectual knowledge and the building of character. Why is this important? Well, think about the many corrupt, yet educated folks in government, business and other arenas. Such people are often successful only for a short season because their character cannot sustain them. Our character, or nature, is entirely important to our growth in any area of life. It is a tying thread upon which many other factors hang.

There are a lot of things that humans fail to take a stand on. The most important matter on which we can take a stand on is our very own life. Dr. Martin Luther King described this well when he said, "Our lives begin to end the day we are silent about things that matter." Our lives matter but do really begin to end the day we fail to take a stand on what we believe. However, it is not very easy to take a stand on issues if we, ourselves, do not know what we stand for.

Sokola njimbu muhinyi mukawana – A.A.M Makai

This is a wonderful nugget of wisdom from my father. Its literal translation is *carry the axe, you can make the handle anywhere.* It refers to issues of choosing the best thing to do. In essence, carry your character; you can make everything else anywhere. I dare you! Carry that character...

Chapter Five

Something attempted, something done,
has earned a night's repose – Henry
Wadsworth Longfellow

To accomplish great things, we must
not only act but also dream; not only
plan but also believe
– Anatole France

Processionary caterpillars travel in long, undulating lines, one creature behind another. Jean-Henri Fabre, a famed French naturalist who died in 1915, once led a group of these caterpillars onto the rim of a large flowerpot, so that the lead caterpillar actually touched the last caterpillar in the procession, forming a complete circle. In the center of the flowerpot Fabre placed pine needles, a main source of food for such creatures. With an ample supply of food close at hand and plainly visible, for seven days and nights the caterpillars circled the flowerpot until they died from exhaustion and starvation. Why? Because these mentally programmed creatures refused to veer off the beaten path. They confused activity with accomplishment[1]...

Many of us seeking to be successful are like these caterpillars – we have been mentally conditioned to walk in circles while our favorite food is less than an inch away. Harold Taylor says that the roots of true achievement lie in the will to become the best that you can become. Many people want to be successful without having the *will* to become the best they can become. In essence, in the lives of many people, the success they have achieved is merely a shadow of *true* success.

The processionary caterpillars work by imitation. The caterpillar behind the first did not find it odd that it could sense the food because it was imitating the lead caterpillar, which was, in turn, imitating the caterpillar it was following. Accomplishment, activity and imitation are very similar to the untrained eye; it takes insight and wisdom to distinguish between them.

No man was ever great by imitation – Samuel Johnson

Many of us have failed to exploit our potential because we have been following a lead caterpillar. Habitual patterns and ways of thinking sometimes become deeply established, and it is more natural to perpetuate these unfruitful patterns than to instigate change – even when change can lead to freedom and achievement. It is difficult for people to realize that just because large numbers of their peers believe or act a certain way, it does not mean that those beliefs or actions are, in fact, the best way of doing things.

Throughout recorded history, when it comes to the subject of achievement and progress, this one idea holds true: *The crowd is always wrong!*

Consider Nazi Germany. Were the Germans right in trying to annihilate the Jews? And here in the United States? Was the inhuman sale and holding of blacks justified because everyone was doing it? As my parents always told me, just because everyone jumps into a ditch doesn't mean you have to do it too.

I often wonder what happened to originality and creativity. Why do I really want a big house on the beach and a sleek BMW? Is it because *I* want it, or because it will measure up with what "they" all have? Sometimes I get tickled when I see how people often conform to the norms of society in order to blend in. Nowadays it is almost a rite of passage for the noveau-riche to buy a home so large it could house a family ten times larger than their own, with space to spare!

We all have different reasons for wanting to be financially successful and secure. Some want the money to be able to afford to party every weekend, while others may want money to build youth facilities in Third World countries. Whatever your motivation, it is essential that you find your own *unique* definition of success and that you lay out the reasons behind your desire to attain such success. Not to discourage anyone, but energy exerted in one quest may be well suited for a totally different quest.

Many a success is nothing but repetitions and counterfeits. If Alexander Graham Bell thought as we do in this day and age, I do not believe that we would be dedicating the phone to his name.

Imitation is the sincerest of flattery –Charles Caleb Colton

All we seem to ever do is imitate instead of initiate! What a shame to wake up each day and work towards being like someone else! The only person we should be working towards being like is Jesus. Everyone and everything else is just earthly and temporal, in other words a total waste of time. What would you do differently if you woke up one day and decided to initiate rather than imitate?

Sadly, even the church has been reduced to copying. I am sick and tired of marveling at the experiences of Saul on the road to Damascus, Moses on Mount Sinai and Peter walking on the water. If we who are called by His name will begin to initiate rather than imitate, a wave of God's glory will wash over this world.

Some people like to be different and outlandish, using mundane reasoning to cover up their foolishness. This is not the sort of initiating behavior that I am referring to. What I propose requires a sound mind and actions motivated by love.

Creative thought is the only power that can produce wealth from a formless substance

The real challenge and the real reward is to take who you are and what you are capable of doing and create the means to achieve your dreams – Carl Mays

CREATIVE CONCEPTS[2]

It had no form and was void when He decided to turn this nothing into something; dampening the words of King Lear in Shakespeare's tragedy *King Lear* – "nothing can come of nothing," – He turned nothing into something. Filled with darkness, He called out light and light obediently presented herself. Pleased with what He saw, He took one look at the water and called out for it to divide itself and set boundaries between itself and the land. As the light, obediently the water divided itself. Impressed with His ingenuity, He spoke to the seeds in the earth to spring forth all manner of life, fruit and herb. Obediently, grass covered the earth and all manner of fruit and vegetation presented itself as commanded. This greatly pleased Him so He then proceeded to call two "lights" into being: the moon and the sun. To accompany these, He spoke to small twinkly stars and they too obediently presented themselves. He then spoke all manner of fish to present themselves in the waters of the earth, all manner of beast and creeping thing upon the land and all manner of fowl of the air. What He did after is most extraordinary and intriguing…

He conferred with *Himself* and decided to make a man *in His own image*. He formed him of the dust of the earth and breathed *Zoë*, the breath of life, into him and behold, he became a living soul. He gave the man dominion over everything upon and under the earth. Finally, He planted a garden in the east and called it Eden. In it was planted every good fruit of the earth, and through it ran four rivers. The land was lush and fertile, covered with gold and precious stones. Into this prepared world did He place Adam of the dust and his wife Eve...

To achieve the marvelous, it is precisely the unthinkable that must be thought – Tom Robbins

It is necessary to grasp the creative nature and concept of God. That same nature and concept is *in* you. Because of your kinship to God, *you* can call those things which be not as if they were (Romans 4:17). Before creation, there was nothing – this thing that God did had never been done before. But when He began to call those things which were not as if they were, things began to happen: molecules and atoms began to collide and form the water, the air and the fish. If you are going to do something spectacular with your life, you are going to need to get off your hind and call those things which be not as if they were – be creative!

> They seized Him in a secluded garden after his betrayer planted a cold kiss on His cheek. They tore off His clothes and beat Him. They spat on Him, mocked Him and hurled insults at Him. They placed a crown of thorns upon His head and ordered Him to carry His cross to Calvary's hill. As He did so, they whipped Him and told Him to keep moving. They placed Him on the cross he had carried and drove nails in His wrists and feet. Upon the raising of His cross, His blood began to run down towards the earth...

With every drop of Jesus' blood, victory came to you and I. Victory over sin and death! Victory over poverty! His precious blood paid all our debts and bought us life everlasting; life that includes financial, social, intellectual and spiritual success and prosperity. Why then, must we live in lack? It's all in our mind! Joshua Smith, founder and C.E.O. of Maxima, said, "Poverty is a state of mind. It's a negative force that numbs the body and drains the spirit."

With all the riches you now possess, why should you live in spiritual *or* financial poverty? Living that way makes Jesus' death by broken heart a complete waste! You *must* realize that the first step to a successful and prosperous life is first realizing that you *are* God's child, predestinated for greatness and bursting at the seams with potential. The Apostle Paul, in his letter to the Church at Ephesus, addressed this when he said:

> Blessed be the God and father of our Lord Jesus Christ, who hath blessed us with all spiritual blessings in heavenly places in Christ; according as he hath chosen us in Him before the foundation of the world, that we should be holy and without blame before Him in love; having predestinated us unto the adoption of children by Jesus Christ to Himself, according to the pleasure of His will – Ephesians 1:3-5

All that Paul was trying to say is that we have the essential ingredients, all we have to do is realize it and work from there. We have already been blessed in heavenly places and we must now use these blessings to bring out the best in ourselves. As Dr. Dennis Kimbro said, "our Creator's work is finished, but the work of creating a better you has just began. For as long as you continue drawing breath, you have the opportunity to complete that work." It is time for you to take a stand and begin to create the life you deserve and want.

The roots of true achievement lie in the will to become the best that you can become – Harold Taylor

Thomas Edison once explained his creativity by saying, "Genius is 1 percent inspiration and 99 percent perspiration." Many studies of creativity show that "genius" and "eminence" owe as much to persistence and dedication as they do to inspiration. You are not dumb or stupid. If you will simply dedicate yourself to hard work, you can begin to develop a creative mind, attitude and concept.

Chapter Six

Experts have pointed out that the average individual conjures up at least four ideas a year, any of which would lead to a modest fortune

If you have but one wish, let it be for an idea – Percy Sutton

TAP INTO YOUR WEALTH AND ACT ON YOUR IDEAS

I seem to have a morbid desire for finding peace and solace at cemeteries. This is because it is there that one will find stories untold, songs unsung, plans and ideas unimplemented, sermons not preached, dreams never realized.

I'm sure you've heard the story about the boilermaker: The boilermaker was contracted by a company to fix a broken boiler. He looked at the boiler, examined the piping, removed his hammer, tapped a pipe, and the boiler began to work. He wrote the bill and gave it to the relevant official who, upon reading it, exclaimed, "Two thousand dollars! You were in there no more than ten minutes!" The boilermaker then broke the bill down as follows:

Tapping with hammer: $0001.00
Knowing where to tap: $1999.00
Total: $2000.00

It is clear from this story that one must know *where* to tap in order for success to be triggered. Too many people are trying to tap on the wrong pipe because they do not know what they are doing.

Often suggestions in the workplace or among friends are turned down with a cursory "that's a bad idea." I urge you to try, by all means necessary, to refrain from viewing an *inappropriate* idea as a bad idea. There is *no* such thing as a bad idea! Many fail to achieve their goals because they are told that their idea is a bad idea. Tap into your idea and don't listen when others criticize you. Then see if you'll soar like an eagle over the ocean or do a belly flop!

Many of the greatest achievers began by having an idea and then acting upon it. In fact, "great" inventions have come about through very simple ideas. Alexander Graham Bell had an idea that resulted in the first telephone. He started out trying to make a hearing aid for his wife and instead invented the telephone! Nelson Mandela had an idea that resulted in the end of apartheid in South Africa. Kenneth David Kaunda had an idea that resulted in the end of colonization and ushered in independence for the nation of Zambia. What ideas do you have?

Nothing in this world is so powerful as an idea whose time has come ~ Victor Hugo

Victor Hugo, a French poet and playwright wrote: "Nothing in this world is so powerful as an idea whose time has come." Some of the greatest men and women in this world began their journey towards success with an idea. In fact, Percy Sutton, owner of the famed Apollo Theater in New York City, once advised that "if you have but one wish, let it be for an idea." His idea to start this world-renowned theater brought him success and fame. What ideas are *you* holding back?

I am convinced that people who are dreamers are, to some extent, more likely than others to be successful. Before I finally got accepted into college in the United States, there were many critics, naysayers and doubters. In fact, they thought my goals and dreams were totally far-fetched. But I had to *see* myself and imagine walking the halls of academia, before the reality could be manifested. Imagination is a success-providing tool that many fail to use. Psychologist and best selling author, Charles Garfield once said, "Ideas are the primary tools needed in constructing a powerful mission. Great accomplishments are always the result of the imagination translated through words and action plans."

Man's mind stretched to a new idea never goes back to its original dimensions ~ Oliver Wendell Holmes

THE IMPORTANCE OF IMAGINATION

Imagination is more important than knowledge ~ Einstein

The word "imagination" comes from the root word *imagine*, which comes from the Latin word *imaginatum[1]*. This word, in turn, comes from *imago[2]*, which means "image." To imagine, therefore, is to form a notion or idea (an image) of something in the mind, or to bring something (an image) before the mind's eye. It follows, then, that *imagination is the faculty or power of the mind to conceive and form ideas (images) of things [which have been communicated to it by sensory information][3]*.

Throughout time, ideas and imagination have been shunned like the plague. However, some of the greatest inventions and success stories come from men and women who have chosen to move forward in their lives and move ideas (created through imagination) from the walls of their mind to reality. Now, for any imaginative thought to prosper in the natural, it must first prosper in the spiritual. This means that one's mind must be attuned to the quest at hand and must be in disregard of the thoughts, intents and criticisms of the world.

Laurence Olivier was earnestly advised by a sincere theatrical expert to give up plans for a career in the theater because he just did not have what it took to be a good actor. If you are familiar with Laurence Olivier's career, you will note that imagination and dreams turned the tables for Laurence Olivier.

This criticism is not limited to the weak-minded, but to those who lead brilliant lives as well. For example, Thomas Edison is on record as having said that talking pictures would never catch on. "Nobody," he said, "would pay to listen to sounds coming from a screen." He also tried to persuade Henry Ford to abandon his work on the fledging idea of a motorcar. "It's a worthless idea," Edison, persistent in his own endeavors, told the young Ford. "Come and work for me and do something really worthwhile."

Ideas are the primary tools needed in constructing a powerful mission. Great accomplishments are always the result of the imagination translated through words and action plans – Charles Garfield

During the early 1900's an impressive array of scientific wizards pooh-poohed the idea of the airplane. "Stuff and nonsense," they said, "An opium-induced fantasy – a crackpot idea."

One of America's most influential scientific journalists hurried to say, "Time and money is being wasted on aircraft experimentation."

One week later, the Wright Brothers taxied their crackpot idea down a homemade runway and launched the human race into the air on a bumpy field in Kitty Hawk, North Carolina.

Even after that, the experts continued to snipe at the idea of air travel. Marshall Foch, Supreme Commander of the Allied Forces in France in World War I, watched a display and said, "All very well for sport, but it is no use whatsoever to the Army."

You tell me: what was used in World War II? Clearly, the Wright brothers' "crackpot idea" revolutionized battle, travel and the global culture.

Even Columbus had trouble financing his ships and convincing a crew to sail "around" the world. Why? Because he was fighting a cultural trance. Most of the people believed that the earth was flat, and were not open to other possibilities. Fortunately, Isabella, Ferdinand and Columbus himself ignored the experts. The *Nina*, the *Pinta* and the little *Santa Maria* set sail, and a flat world was found to be round. "Impossible" new lands became thriving and very "possible" places. This was because Columbus conjured up some ideas through imagination and now his name remains in the annals of history.

Hold nothing back, my friend. There is *no* such thing as a bad idea!

Chapter Seven

Courage is resistance to fear, mastery of fear, not absence of fear
– Mark Twain

In Southwest Asia during the 14th century, the army of Asian conqueror Emperor Tamerlane, a descendant of Genghis Khan, was routed and dispersed by a powerful enemy. Emperor Tamerlane himself lay hidden in a deserted manger while enemy troops scoured the countryside looking for him.

As he lay there, desperate and dejected, Tamerlane watched an ant try to carry a grain of corn over a perpendicular wall. The kernel was larger than the ant itself. As the emperor counted, sixty-nine times the ant tried to carry it up the wall. Sixty-nine times he fell back. On the seventieth try he pushed the grain of corn over the top. Tamerlane leaped to his feet with a shout! He, too, would triumph in the end! And he did, by reorganizing his forces and putting the enemy to flight.

The word courage is French and descends from the Latin root *cor*, which means *the heart*. Courageous men and women have big hearts, and though they may fall dozens of times while trying to do something quite impossible, like walk up a wall, they try and try again, refusing to be brought down.

Courage is the instrument by which the hero realizes himself – Beowulf

In the epic poem *Beowulf*, the great warrior Beowulf points out so wonderfully that courage is the instrument by which the hero realizes himself. The greatest men in battle are those with limitless courage. David slew Goliath the giant through courage, Joshua conquered Canaan through courage and Jesus Christ defeated the devil through courage.

In the books of Deuteronomy and Joshua, which chronicles the passing down of the leadership mantle from Moses to Joshua, the word courage is used numerous times, notably in conjunction with the admonition to "be strong." Joshua is told by the Lord *three* times to be courageous and *twice* by Moses to be courageous because the task that lay before him was going to require great fortitude. Why three times by God and twice by Moses? Was or is courage such a big deal that it had to be told him five times? Let us look closer...

Deuteronomy 31:6 – Be strong and of a good courage...

Deuteronomy 31:7 – And Moses called unto Joshua, and said to him in the sight of all Israel, "Be strong and of a good courage…"
Joshua 1:6 – Be strong and of a good courage…
Joshua 1:7 – Only be strong and very courageous…
Joshua 1:9 – Have I not commanded thee? Be strong and of a good courage…

Joshua was first told to be courageous as Moses spoke to the entire nation of Israel (Deut. 31:6) then "in the sight of all Israel" in verse seven. Then "after the death of Moses, the servant of the Lord, it came to pass that the Lord spake unto Joshua" and told him to be courageous three times. What is key to understand in this narrative is the fact that Joshua and Israel were about to walk into their destiny – the Promised Land.

I can hear God telling you and I: *Be strong and of a good courage.* It is when we are at the threshold of entering into our rest and our promise that we need the most courage; however, this is generally the time our courage fails us and we become wobbly in our legs, nervous and fearful. However, "be not afraid, neither be thou dismayed for the Lord thy God is with thee withersoever thou goest" (Joshua 1:9). God told Joshua that He would not fail him or forsake him. Moses told Joshua that God would go before him, God would be with him, and He would not fail him.

Courage is an essential ingredient to success. Without the courage to do the things we have been called to do, we cannot possibly accomplish them. Most of the ideas that we conjure up never see fruition because we become discouraged and realize that we cannot do it. The truth is that *we* cannot do it, except that the Lord be with us and go before us.

Greatness is buried within your heart but you must muster the courage to mine it out – Bessie Pender

How many people have failed to realize their God-given gifts and talents because they did not have the courage they needed! The world will judge you and place you in certain categories from which you must depart. Some very intelligent young people have been discouraged from going to college because they already have a good job and because mom and dad made it without much formal education, so they can do it too. Some potentially great musicians have been discouraged because their friends in the neighborhood would laugh at them if they saw them carrying a violin or a cello. Some potentially powerful preachers and ministers have been discouraged because they did not fit into the "proper" profile of what a minister should be like…

Correction does much, but encouragement does more
– Johann Wolfgang Von Goethe

The entire purpose of this book is to be a tool to encourage those that are down and, through personal experience, show them that all things are possible. Indeed, correction does much but encouragement does more because if I encourage you at *your* level, you will go even higher.

I have no doubt that, just as Joshua was, you are faced with some great challenges in your life. You may not have the resources that others have been blessed with, you may not have the knack for certain things that others do but if you look deep enough and long enough, you will see that you have a knack for something unique and valuable and possess certain resources that you can use to realize your God-given destiny.

7 KEYS TO GREATER COURAGE

CONVICTION: Concentrate on the things in which your conviction outmatches your circumstances. Remember: *One man with conviction is stronger than 100 with only an interest or desire.*

ORGANIZATION: There is nothing that brings confusion to the mind like disorder in your physical world. If you are failing to maintain an organized home, car or office, you may be an easy target for discouragement. However, I realize that organization is subjective: a friend of mine in Zambia had ALL his clothes on the floor in his bedroom, but if you asked him where something was, he would fish it out with one stroke! However, if one cannot use the wardrobes in one's room then it might be tough for that person to use the gifts

65

endowed to him from the foundation of the earth. Remember: *If you are faithful over a few, God will make you ruler over more.*

UNITY OF MIND: The book of James says that a double-minded man is unstable in all his ways. To your conviction and organization, add single-mindedness and set your heart on one thing – the threshold in question. Remember, *tis' the mind that makes the body rich.*

RESPONSIBILITY: You must begin to be responsible for what you allow to move you and stir you up. When you allow the wrong people to have influence in your life, you can count on your victory turning into defeat and disgrace. Remember, as Abraham Lincoln once stated: *You cannot escape the responsibility of tomorrow by evading it today.*

AWARENESS OF MIND: Coupled with unity of mind, having awareness of mind will allow you to be alert, ready for anything that has the potential to discourage you or set you back in your quest for greater courage, strength and success. Remember, as Gandhi said, *The real seat of taste is not the tongue but the mind.*

GOD: God is the One that ensures your success and ability to stand strong. This should have been the first point mentioned but for practical purposes, it comes sixth. You *must* allow God in to let Him do what He does best. Remember the words of Ralph Waldo Emerson: *God enters by a private door into every individual.*

EARNESTNESS: Being honest with yourself will make you more courageous. Do not try to be tough like a coconut when being soft like a tomato would be more appropriate. You can sin behind closed doors and foolishly lie to others about how holy you are. But remember, you are a fool when you lie to yourself. Remember, in the words of Blaise Pascal, that *earnestness is enthusiasm tempered by reason.*

Courage consists not in blindly overlooking danger, but in meeting it with eyes open – Jean Paul Richter

Perhaps this acronym will become a tool that you can use to have more courage, and to see that courage has more to do with your heart than you might think. Work on developing a big heart and seeing the good in the bad, the light in the dark, the joy in the sadness, the faith in the doubt. Emulate the prayer of St. Francis of Assisi:

Lord, make me an instrument of your peace
Where there is hatred...let me sow love
Where there is injury...pardon
Where there is doubt...faith
Where there is despair...hope
Where there is darkness...light
Where there is sadness...joy
O Divine Master, grant that I may not so much seek
To be consoled...as to console
To be understood...as to understand
To be loved...as to love
For
It is in giving...that we receive
It is in pardoning...that we are pardoned
It is in dying...that we are born to eternal life.

A brave man struggling with adversity is a spectacle for the gods
~ Seneca

One of the most interesting perspectives on courage is depicted in a story I once read about the 1800 United States frontier:

> In the late 1800's, a salesman from back east arrived at a frontier town somewhere on the Great Plains. As he was talking to the owner of a general store, a rancher came in, and the owner excused himself to take care of his customer. As they talked, the salesman couldn't help overhearing their conversation. It seemed the rancher wanted credit for some things he needed.
> "Are you doing any fencing this spring, Jake?" asked the storekeeper.
> "Sure am, Bill," said the rancher.
> "Fencing in or fencing out?"
> "Fencing in. Taking in another three hundred and sixty acres across the creek."

67

"Good to hear it, Jake. You got the credit. Just tell Steve out back what you need."

The salesman was dumbfounded. "I've seen all kinds of credit systems," he said, "but never one like that. How does it work?"

"Well," said the storekeeper, "let me tell you. If a man's fencing out, that means he's scared, trying to just hold on to what he's got. But if he's fencing in, he's growing and trying to improve. I always give credit to a man who's fencing in because that means he believes in himself."[1]

People of courage believe in themselves and refuse to be deterred by naysayers and attacks by the enemy. I have met many people whom I have had to handle with leather gloves lest I get a splinter in my finger from the chip on their shoulders! They carry their emotions on their shoulders, and the smallest of resistance can trigger the water works in their eyes, and uncertainty in their hearts.

To be forewarned is to be forearmed – Bruce Carroll

Bruce Carroll, my biology professor, constantly told me that to be forewarned is to be forearmed. Anticipated, impending danger or trouble is far easier to handle than that which is unexpected.

Take Noah and his family for example. They prepared ahead of time for the impending floods while others were doing their own thing. I can imagine the fun that was poked at them, but we all know who had the last laugh.

Most of what is worthwhile and meaningful lies on the other side of our comfort zone. Success, be it spiritual, financial or otherwise, is not for sissies or the lilly-livered; it belongs to men and women that have developed a knack for revolutionizing their lives and becoming all that they can be. Life is not about what we wear, what we eat or what we want; life is all about *becoming* what God wants us to be. If we do not *become*, we do not live; if we do not live, we serve no purpose on earth. Like every manufacturer builds things with a particular use intended, you were built with *divine intent*! But you must muster the courage, get off your hind, spare us the sob stories and make something of yourself!

Courage is not simply one of the virtues, but the form of every virtue at the testing point – C.S Lewis

A man once found a plump cocoon in which a butterfly was growing. One day the man noticed a small opening, and he sat and watched the cocoon for several hours as the butterfly struggled to force its body out through the tiny hole. Then it seemed to stop making any progress. It appeared as if it had gotten as far as it could and was unable to go any farther. So the man decided to help the butterfly. He took a pair of scissors and snipped the remaining bit of the cocoon. The butterfly then emerged easily. But something was not right. The butterfly had a swollen body and shriveled wings. The man continued to watch the butterfly because he expected at any moment, the wings would enlarge and expand to be able to support the body, which would contract in time. Neither happened. In fact, the butterfly spent the rest of its life crawling around with a swollen body and deformed wings. It was never able to fly. What the man in his kindness and haste did not understand, was that the restricting cocoon and the struggle required for the butterfly to get through the small opening of the cocoon were God's way of forcing fluid from the body of the butterfly into its wings so that it would be ready for flight once it achieved its freedom from the cocoon. Sometimes struggles are exactly what we need in our life. If God allowed us to go through all our life without any obstacles, that would cripple us; we would not be as strong as what we could have been. Not only that, we could never fly[2].

God has put all people on this earth to accomplish certain things. Some are so behind, they are never going to die!

I have now realized that lack of courage is a great thief of time and success. Sometimes life is filled with much pain, misery and strife but life must go on. It is up to us to take steps to ensure that we do not cower at the first sign of resistance or trouble. Here is an inspiring poem called *It's All Up To You*[3].

If you think you're a winner you'll win,

If you dare to step out you'll succeed
Believe in your heart, have a purpose to start

Aim to help fellow man in his need

Thoughts of faith must replace every doubt
Use words of courage and you cannot fail
If you stumble and fall,
Rise and stand ten feet tall
You determine the course that you sail

For in life as in death don't you see
It's the man who has nothing to fear
Who approaches the gates,
Stands a moment and waits
Feels the presence of God oh so near

You've been given the power to see
What it takes to be a real man
Let your thinking be pure, it will make you secure
If you want to, you know that you can

Courage is all about the heart that you have. You *must* be able to stand the pressures of life in order to become the creature God created you to be. There can never be any becoming without courage.

An Anonymous author wrote the following poem called *Risking*:

To laugh is to risk appearing the fool.
To weep is to risk appearing sentimental.
To reach out for another is to risk involvement.

To expose feeling is to risk exposing your true self
To place your ideas, your dreams, before the crowd is
to risk their loss
To love is to risk not being loved in return
To live is to risk dying
To hope is to risk despair
To try is to risk failure

Courage would never be necessary without there being a risk in living and becoming. With all the risks outlined above, is it not obvious that we must look adversity in the face and fight? Is it not obvious that we must face the reality of what we do and hold tight? I challenge you to become...

Chapter Eight

Any desire that you plant deeply in your subconscious will eventually seek expression through the physical world

There is something phenomenally invigorating about watching an individual expressing a will to live. Whatever resource is afforded him, he uses it to sustain himself and survive. Those that seek success are like such individuals – treasuring and maximizing the next breath.

Desire and initiative, when properly applied, lead to growth and development

Dennis Kimbro, in *What Makes the Great Great*, tells the story of Phil Knight, a mediocre miler on the track team in college whose best time for the event was four minutes and thirteen seconds.

> Knight had trained under the watchful eye of Bill Bowerman, the renowned University of Oregon track coach. During the late 1950's, Bowerman's training techniques placed little known Eugene, Oregon, on the map when, year after year, he turned out a bevy of world-record-setting long-distance runners. In an effort to improve the times of his athletes, he toyed with running shoes. Their improvement became his silent passion. This innovative coach had theorized that slicing even an ounce off a runner's cleats might just prove the critical difference between winning and losing.
>
> While completing an MBA at Stanford University, Knight wrote a research paper based on his theory that the Japanese could do for athletic shoes what they had done for cameras. Convinced by his ideas, Knight took off for Japan, hoping to corner the domestic rights for Tiger running shoes. Upon returning home, he shared samples with his ex-coach as they made plans to set up shop. In 1964, Knight and Bowerman each scraped together $500 and formed the Blue Ribbon Sports Company, sole U.S. distributor of Tiger equipment. Strapped for cash, Knight placed their small inventory in his father-in-law's basement and peddled his wares at night and on weekends to

high school athletic teams. By year's end, sales had approached $8,000. Although this was hardly enough profit for him to justify quitting his full-time accounting job, Knight's dream rested on larger goals. He knew he was a big fish in a small pond. The sport shoe market was new, wide open, and seemingly inexhaustible.

Adidas, a West German corporation, had been the innovator in athletic equipment up to this point. Although the European firm had set the standard that was subsequently followed by most of its competitors, it had drastically misjudged the potential and opportunity of the 1970 athletic boom. Even U.S. manufacturers like Converse and Keds were caught napping. Knight and Bowerman could hardly sit still. The next year, in 1971, they gambled everything and decided to go after a large share of the American market by developing their own shoe.

Bowerman, ever the tinkerer, fashioned a waffle ironed urethane rubber piece to produce a more durable, cushioned sole. The new "waffle shoe" proved popular and exceeded expectations. Pushing full blast, they contracted much of the work abroad to mostly Asian factories, adopted the "swoosh" logo, and called their product *Nike*, after the Greek goddess of victory. In 1980, *Nike* went public, shooting Knight's net worth to $300 million. Bowerman, who had long since retired, sold most of his stock and opted for a more relaxed lifestyle far removed from corporate boardrooms and shoe wars...

You cannot blaze forth unless the fire has been smoldered within you – Carol Moseley Braun

Phil Knight and Bill Bowerman saw what those of a lesser vision didn't see and rode the crest of a booming industry. It is undeniable that the world we live in today is not an easy one – turmoil, broken homes, and forgotten morals are but a drop in the ocean of troubles that life today offers.

I remember the long discussions I had with my father before I left Zambia and moved to the United States. Having failed once before to make the move, and lacking the financial resources I needed, it took me about six months to convince him to give me his blessing and let me go. Though he presented sound, rational reasons for me to stay in Zambia, I was determined to make it in the United States, and would not give up on my dreams. Bottom line: He blessed me and allowed me to do it because I would not let up.

PERSISTENCE: THE VEHICLE THAT TRANSFORMS FAILURE INTO SUCCESS

A plaque in the kinesiology building of my old college reads:

> Nothing in the world can take the place of persistence. Talent will not; nothing is more common than unsuccessful men with talent. Genius will not; unrewarded genius is almost a proverb. Education will not; the world is full of educated derelicts. Persistence and determination alone are omnipotent.

These words, spoken by the former United States President Calvin Coolidge, opened my eyes to the world of what Dr. John C. Maxwell calls *failing forward*. Failing forward is simply turning mistakes into stepping stones for success[1]. Too many people have failed to realize and maximize their potential because they are not persistent. You see, giving up and giving in to failure is the line of least resistance. Many dreams and goals have been abandoned when all that was needed was the last mile.

When a man's fight begins within himself, he is worth something – Robert Browning

We seem to be faced with a tragic situation in which many people do not have enough fight in them to become all that they are destined to be. Like Ali Hafed and the Golconda diamond mine, they give up too soon. What is the problem then? They have never been sold on the idea of "keepin' on keepin' on." Therefore, their desires soon wane and become just another dream that didn't work out, when they may have attained the prize had they stuck it out a little while longer.

Don't miss your opportunity! So many people go through life regretting not having "stuck it out" at some time or another. It is time for you to stand up and refuse to back down when the going gets tough. Jesus stated:

> Enter ye in at the strait gate; for wide is the gate and broad is the way that leadeth to destruction; and many there be which go in thereat. Because strait is the gate and narrow is the way which leadeth unto life; and few there be that find it (Matthew 7:13-14)

The way towards destruction and giving up is wide – hence many people take that route. However, the way towards life and success – and "keepin' on keepin' on" – is narrow and, indeed, very few find it. I pray you would seek the narrow road.

There is not a single problem on this earth that is beyond solution. Be encouraged. You *can* become the person that God has called you to be. I challenge you to fight with everything that you've got!

Chapter Nine

There is nothing noble in being
superior to some other man. True
nobility is in being superior to
your precious self
– Hindu proverb

In our day and age, one's integrity, character and hunger determine how successful one will be in life. The thread upon which each of these characteristics lies is discipline; the discipline to strive until one succeeds, the discipline to control oneself when appropriate and the discipline to learn to discipline oneself. *Longman's Dictionary of the English Language* defines "discipline" as "to train or develop by instruction and exercise." There can be no development or progress without discipline because *every* fundamental aspect of life involves discipline. I have found, in my research and personal experience that desire, determination, diligence, and drive are factors that directly influence discipline.

Desire and initiative, when properly applied lead to growth and development

"Any desire that you plant deeply in your subconscious will eventually seek expression through the physical world," wrote Dr. Dennis Kimbro in his book *What Makes the Great Great.* Longman's dictionary defines desire as "a *conscious* impulse towards an object or experience that promises enjoyment or satisfaction" (emphasis mine). To be disciplined, one must consciously decide to do so, and that decision must be fueled by a desire to accomplish the intended goal. The nineteenth Century English poet, Robert Browning, noted: *When a man's fight begins within himself, he is worth something.* The fight must most certainly begin within you if you are going to accomplish your goals. It *is* all about you! Boxing mogul, Don King once said, "If you set yourself on fire, the world will come see you burn." It is absolutely essential to understand that without desire one cannot become disciplined and move towards progress and development because, as Dr. Kimbro said, "Desire and initiative, when properly applied lead to growth and development."

You may not be responsible for getting knocked down, but you're certainly responsible for getting back up

According to the theory of aerodynamics the bumblebee should be unable to fly. Because of its size, weight and shape in relationship to its total wingspan, flying is scientifically impossible. However, the bumblebee is apparently ignorant of such scientific theory and thus goes ahead and flies anyway; the bumblebee flies every day of its life by sheer determination. Determination is the power or habit of deciding definitely or firmly. As Reverend Jesse Jackson said, "You may not be responsible for getting knocked down, but you're certainly responsible for getting back up." There is in this world no greater force than the force of a man or woman determined to rise!

Few things are impossible to diligence. Great works are performed not by strength, but perseverance – Samuel Johnson

Longman's dictionary defines diligence as "steady application and effort." Experts say that it takes twenty-one days for one to learn or adopt a habit; therefore, steady application and effort affords the opportunity to work on aspects of discipline. "Few things are impossible to diligence. Great works are performed not by strength, but perseverance," wrote Samuel Johnson.

"All of your scholarship, all of your study of Shakespeare and Wordsworth would be in vain if at the same time you did not build your character and attain mastery over your thoughts and your actions," said Mahatma Gandhi to a group of college students. Longman's dictionary defines *drive* as "great zeal in the pursuance of one's ends." An old proverb says: *Zeal is like fire; it needs both feeding and watching.* One must have drive in order for one to be disciplined. Without drive, discipline is impossible.

VINCE LOMBARDI: AN EXAMPLE OF DRIVE[1]

I've never known a man worth his salt who in the long run, deep down in his heart, didn't appreciate the grind, the discipline. There is something good in men that really yearns for discipline – Vince Lombardi

Vincent Thomas Lombardi was born on June 11, 1913 in Brooklyn, New York. He was the first of Henry and Matilda Lombardi's five children. Raised in the Catholic faith, Vincent studied the priesthood for two years before transferring to St. Frances Preparatory High School, where he was a star fullback on the football team. In 1933 he was accepted at New York City's Fordham University and after a year on the freshman team, the 170-pound sophomore guard was put into Fordham's steadfast defensive line, which was tagged the "Seven Blocks of Granite." Vincent not only proved to be a success on the field but off the field as well, graduating magna cum laude in business in 1937.

After working for a finance company and playing semi-pro football with Delaware's Wilmington Clippers, he took a teaching and coaching job at St. Cecilia High School in Englewood, New Jersey. For $1,700 a year he taught Latin, algebra, physics and chemistry, and coached the football, basketball and baseball teams. In 1949, Earl "Colonel Red" Blaik, football coach for the United States Military Academy at West Point (and considered the best coach in the country at the time), hired Vince to manage their varsity defensive line. Working seventeen-hour days with Blaik, whose expertise helped refine his leadership skills, Vince was taught to stick with clear-cut plays (simple blocking and tackling), strive for perfect execution and conduct himself respectfully on the field.

In 1954, Vince left West Point for an assistant coaching position with the New York Giants, under head coach and former classmate Jim Lee Howell. Vince was in charge of offensive strategy for the Giants, while future Dallas Cowboys coach Tom Landry led the defense. The previous season, the Giants suffered with a 3-9 record and scored the least number of points in the entire league. Within three years of Vince's arrival, however, the Giants become a championship team. His leadership and discipline brought out the talents of football great Frank Gifford, whom he switched from defense to offense. For each of the five years that Vince coached the Giants, Gifford was nominated as a halfback on the all-pro team.

Mental toughness is many things and rather difficult to explain. Its qualities are sacrifice and self-denial. Also, most importantly, it is combined with a perfectly disciplined will that refuses to give

in. It's a state of mind – you could call it character in action.
– Vince Lombardi

In 1958, the 45-year-old coach, having become tired of being an assistant, accepted a challenging five-year contract in Wisconsin as the general manager and head coach of perpetual losers the Green Bay Packers. Having no clout or history in professional football, and the team winning only one game the year before, Vince saw the Packers as a chance to prove himself and his coaching abilities. It has been said that when Vince held the first of his notoriously intense training camps to gear up for the 1959 season, he told the players, "Dancing is a contact sport. Football is a hitting sport." Always expecting obedience, dedication and supreme effort from each man, Vincent promised them that if they obeyed his rules and used his method, they would be a championship team.

Three years later, that promise became a reality. On December 31, 1961, at Lambeau Field in Green Bay, Vince watched proudly as the Packers defeated the New York Giants 37-0 for the National Football League championship.

Though faced with long hours and fierce competition, Vince always put forth nothing less than best effort. Just as he drilled his men to be the paramount players in professional football, he challenged himself by constantly looking to implement new plays and game strategies such as changing his players' jersey numbers before a game to confuse rival teams. His defensive line became so powerful that they were dubbed the "Green Bay Sweep."

After nine phenomenal winning seasons with the Packers, and still serving as general manager, Vince decided to retire as head coach. Under his direction, the Packers had dominated professional football, had collected six division titles, five NFL championships, Super Bowl I & II and acquired a record of 89-29-4. They had become the measuring stick that all other teams tried to emulate – they *became* a discipline.

Less than a year later, however, Vince realized that he still wanted to coach. After being approached by the *Washington Redskins*, he accepted the head coaching position in 1969. Keeping what had become the "Lombardi tradition," he led the Redskins to their first winning record in 14 years. His professional coaching record, unmarred by a losing season, stood at a remarkable 105-35-6 and the NFL named him their acclaimed "1960's Man of the Decade."

The good Lord gave you a body that can stand most anything. It's your mind you have to convince – Vince Lombardi

Sadly, Vince did not have the opportunity to lead another team to the Super Bowl because he was diagnosed with intestinal cancer and died on September 3, 1970. Over 3,500 people from around the country attended his funeral. It has been said that United States President Richard Nixon, who had telegrammed Vince get well wishes while he was ill, sent another telegram of condolence to his wife, Marie, signed "The People."

What is most incredible about Vince is that he helped the men he coached succeed to the furthest of their abilities. Through *discipline*, he brought them pride and victory, and his legacy of perseverance, hard work and dedication has made him one of the most admired and well respected coaches in history.

He was inducted into the Professional Football Hall of Fame in 1971. Considered to be the National Football League's most prestigious award, the Super Bowl trophy was renamed the Vince Lombardi Super Bowl Trophy in his honor. And most recently in 2000, ESPN named him "Coach of the Century."

The mind that is properly disciplined and directed to a clear-cut objective cannot be defeated – Kimbro

The greatest victories in life seem to always come through for men and women who are disciplined. Men and women who have learned to remain focused regardless of the obstacles; men and woman who have developed a personal philosophy of determination and drive. "The first and best victory is for a man to conquer himself," wrote Plato. If we are to be victorious, first we must conquer ourselves because then, and only then, will we be able to accomplish the impossible and become the improbable.

*There is nothing noble in being superior to some other man.
True nobility is in being superior to your precious self
~ Hindu proverb*

Key to any major success story is discipline. Discipline is simply the ability to focus oneself on a set objective and doing the things required to accomplish that objective. Like wisdom, discipline *can* be taught – with the 4.5 whippings per week I got as a child, I can attest to that! It is practically *foolish* for you to think that you can accomplish any feat without discipline.

Discipline has overarching influence in our lives. Many famous, wealthy musicians have found themselves inexplicably bankrupt due to a lack of discipline. A great many potential "Einsteins" have failed out of college because they failed to be disciplined in the area of their studies and academics...and the list goes on. To live life without discipline is to live a life without purpose and conviction. We each need to have self-discipline in order for us to realize the potential that is within us.

*Learn early in life to say, "I can't afford it." It is an
indication of power, courage, and character
~ Benjamin Franklin*

Have you ever met one of those people that never says no? Someone that is always ready to help you? I bet there is one in your office or school or church. Often, such people have failed to discipline themselves in the area of refusal – they are *people pleasers.* They are good old Josies and good old Joes who are good-for-nothing, indisciplined fools. I know that is a strong statement but let the truth be told. Perhaps they lack the understanding, initiative and discipline to be their own man or woman and simply fail at other miniscule tasks because of that. Are you one of those good old Josies or good old Joes? Or perhaps do you know one? Here are four pointers that are helpful in overcoming such a mentality:

♦ Recognize that you have been "fearfully and wonderfully made."

♦ Realize that you can't say yes to everyone all the time
♦ Turn around and tell your past to take a hike
♦ Punish yourself for every foolish yes you say

Discipline interacts with your mindset. Education is a very good opportunity to develop discipline as it constantly requires one to hand in assignments and prepare for quizzes and examinations. Self-education often has positive effects as well. For example, I try to read a minimum of two, 220-page (average) books per week. In order for me to do this while writing a book, being a full time graduate student, working at my church, and speaking across the globe, I must discipline myself to finish those books in the allocated time – as well as all of my other responsibilities.

PROCRASTINATION: THE ENEMY OF DISCIPLINE

Procrastination is the thief of time – Edward Young

I had never heard the word "procrastination" until a few of years ago when a friend used it. I liked the way it was pronounced and liked that it was a long word. So I pondered its meaning – being the self-proclaimed etymologist I am – and searched it out. Procrastination comes from the root word procrastinate. This, in turn, is derived from the Latin words *procrastino*[1] and *procrastinatus*[2]: *pro* means "forward"; *crastinus*[3] means "belonging to the morrow." *Webster's Encyclopedic Dictionary of the English Language* defines procrastination as "the act or habit of putting off to a future time[4]."

Procrastination is like a credit card; it's a lot of fun until you get the bill – Christopher Parker

When you begin to put things off, especially until the last minute, you are always under pressure. That report your boss asked for a fortnight ago should have already been done, but now you're under pressure to have it on his desk by 5pm on Friday and it's now 3:30pm. Does this sound familiar? How about this? That research assignment your instructor gave you at the beginning of the semester is due this

84

afternoon, and you only began working on it this morning? Does this relate to you? All this is only to say, in the words of Christopher Parker, *procrastination is like a credit card; it's a lot of fun until you get the bill.* You may think you can swipe your way through life until you have hit your credit limit but be assured that the bill is on its way!

Discipline is the ability to conquer yourself, set guidelines for yourself to follow, and to appropriate the gifts and abilities already present in you

Plato hit a home run when he wrote: *The first and best victory is for a man to conquer himself.* Discipline is the ability to conquer yourself, set guidelines for yourself to follow, and to appropriate the gifts and abilities already present in you. A lot of folks have failed to realize their goals and maximize their potential because they have failed to conquer themselves and their shortcoming so perhaps it's time for you to get honest with yourself about certain discipline-related shortcomings you may have.

Chapter Ten

In one hand I have a dream, and
in the other I have an obstacle.
Tell me, which one grabs
your attention? – Henry Parks

We all have dreams, as evidenced by a story published on the Internet by family therapist Virginia Satir. She wrote:

> Some years ago I took on an assignment in a southern county to work with people on public welfare. What I wanted to do was show that everybody has the capacity to be self-sufficient, and all we have to do is to activate them. I asked the county to pick a group of people who were on public welfare, people from different racial groups and different family constellations. I would then see them as a group for three hours every Friday. I also asked for a little petty cash to work with, as I needed it.
>
> The first thing I said after I shook hands with everybody was, "I would like to know what your dreams are." Everyone looked at me as if I were kind of wacky. "Dreams? We don't have dreams."
>
> I said, "Well, when you were a kid what happened? Wasn't there something you wanted to do?"
>
> One woman said to me, "I don't know what you can do with dreams. The rats are eating up my kids."
>
> "Oh," I said.
>
> "That's terrible. No, of course, you are very much involved with the rats and your kids. How can that be helped?"
>
> "Well, I could use a new screen door because there are holes in my screen door."
>
> I asked, "Is there anybody around here who knows how to fix a screen door?"
>
> There was a man in the group, and he said, "A long time ago I used to do things like that, but now I have a terribly bad back, but I'll try."
>
> I told him I had some money if he would go to the store, buy some screening, and go and fix the lady's screen door.
>
> "Do you think you can do that?"
>
> "Yes, I'll try."

The next week, when the group was seated, I said to the woman, "Well is your screen door fixed?"

"Oh, yes," she said.

"Then we can start dreaming, can't we?"

She sort of smiled at me.

I said to the man, who did the work, "How do you feel?"

He said, "Well, you know, it's a very funny thing. I'm beginning to feel a lot better."

That helped the group to begin to dream. These seemingly small successes allowed the group to see that dreams were not insane. These small steps began to get people to see and feel that something really could happen.

I began to ask other people about their dreams. One woman shared that she always wanted to be a secretary.

I said, "Well, what stands in your way?" (That's always my next question).

She said, "I have six kids, and I don't have anyone to take care of them while I'm away."

"Let's find out," I said.

"Is there anybody in this group who would take care of six kids for a day or two a week while this woman gets some training here at the community college?"

One woman said, "I got kids, too, but I could do that."

"Let's do it," I said. A plan was created and the woman went to school.

Everyone found something. The man who put in the screen door became a handyman. The woman who took in the children became a licensed foster care person. In 12 weeks I had all these people off public welfare. I've not only done that once, I've done it many times[1].

Dreamers are fine; provided they build foundations under their dreams by working daily towards them ~ Zig Ziglar

What Virginia Satir did was activate this group of people's dreams and allow them to live those dreams. It *is* sad that we think that such a venture is childish, forgetting that we are all the *children* of God of whom He said:

> Suffer little children to come unto me, and forbid them not; for of such is the kingdom of God. Verily I say unto you, whosoever shall not receive the kingdom of God as a little child shall in no wise enter therein. (Luke 18:16-17)

"Dreamers are fine; provided they build foundations under their dreams by working daily towards them," wrote Zig Ziglar. We need to dream, and when we dream, we need to dream BIG. Nineteenth Century writer, James Allen, a great inspiration to me, once wrote:

> Dream lofty dreams, and as you dream so shall you become. Your vision is the promise of what you shall one day be; your ideal is the prophecy of what you shall at last unveil. The greatest achievement was at first and for a time a dream. The oak sleeps in the acorn; the bird waits in the egg; and in the highest vision of the soul a waking angel stirs. Your circumstances may be uncongenial, but they shall not long remain so when you perceive an ideal and strive to reach it.

When we dream big, we also need to set and build deeper foundations. Remember: *the bigger the object, the harder the fall.* If you are currently chasing a big dream, you must ensure that your foundation is deep enough and strong enough to sustain the trouble that comes with big dreams and aspirations. In the words of Anatole France, "To accomplish great things, we must not only act but also dream; not only plan but also believe."

THE FOUNDATION

When I first moved to the United States, I was in awe of the tall buildings and skyscrapers in New York City. Coming from a nation with few tall buildings, I was amazed as I looked all around me at that concrete jungle. It now dawns on me that the foundation for such big dreams (for such buildings were once dreams) must go really deep in order to support such great structures. So it is with our dreams; we must determine how big our dreams are and prepare to set up a foundation strong and deep enough to sustain their structure.

Can you imagine how deep the foundation of the Empire State Building is? Can you imagine what would happen if the foundation was only six feet deep? That building would have toppled during the first phase of construction! If we are to become all that God has called us to be, we must ensure that our roots go so deep that no one can deter us from our dreams. An old oak tree has its roots so deeply and firmly set in the ground that although the rain may come, the storm may rage, and the winds may blow, it stands tall and strong without fail.

In the gospel of Matthew, upon seeing the multitudes, the Master went up on a mountain and taught:

> Therefore whosoever heareth these sayings of mine, and doeth them, I will liken him unto a wise man, which built his house upon a rock. And the rain descended, and the floods came, and the winds blew, and beat upon that house and it fell not for it was founded upon a rock. And every one that heareth these sayings of mine, and doeth them not shall be likened unto a foolish man, which built his house upon the sand. And the rain descended, and the floods came, and the winds blew, and beat upon that house and it fell and great was the fall of it – Matt. 7:24-27

The only difference between the foolish man and the wise man is the site upon which each chose to build his house. The only difference between those that eventually live their dreams and those that do nothing but dream is the site each chooses to build those dreams on. Any successful dreamer will tell you that dreaming was only part of the task because you must "know what your dreams will cost and be willing to pay the price", as Bill Pinkney said.

Everyone has dreams. The key thing to all of this is what we choose to do with our dreams. Some choose to simply have dreams while others choose to build a solid foundation and then lay their dreams upon that foundation.

THE MEMOIRS OF A DREAMER

I was browsing the Internet one morning when I stumbled across the website of Gospel Outreach Fellowship, one of Lusaka's great Pentecostal churches. Having watched the church grow from a tent to a remarkable facility, I decided to email the senior Pastor, Helmut Reutter. As we developed a lengthy correspondence and relationship, I was touched when he wrote:

> Thank you very much for keeping me up to date. I am really touched by your dedication to your home country. I know God will give you great success. I praise God, for the favor He has given you in the place where He sent you. You are a modern day Joseph.

I have held on to those words for the past few years because I know the way Joseph turned out to be – he saved a civilization by heeding to the call of God on his life. The story of Joseph's pampered teen life, near-murder, enslavement, and eventual rise to power offers many lessons to be learned.

Genesis chapter 37 tells the story of Joseph, his relationship with his father and the resentment and animosity between himself and his brothers. From this chapter, we learn some things about having dreams.

And Joseph dreamed a dream, and he told it his brethren and they hated him yet the more (Genesis 37:5)

First of all, not all dreams should be told to everyone. I believe that there are two types of dreams: come-up dreams and give-up dreams. Come-up dreams, as the name suggests, are those dreams that promise a rise in your emotional, financial, spiritual or physical status. Give-up dreams are dreams that project us quitting something: smoking, drinking, anger spurts and the like. Tell your give-up dreams to everything that moves or shows signs of life! It will keep you motivated and accountable. However, be very selective and sensitive when you tell your come-up dreams – especially when it directly involves the person you are telling. If you are vying for a top post like vice president of marketing, don't tell your co-workers in the marketing department that you are going to be the VP of Marketing; they will likely sabotage your dreams and you might end up like Joseph – thrown in a pit and finally sold!

And he dreamed yet another dream... (Genesis 37:9)

The second lesson we are to learn is that irrespective of what others say about you, or do to you, you must *not* stop dreaming. The enemy would just love to see your self-esteem drop like a rock off a cliff, but you *must* transcend the naysayers and haters. After revealing his first dream, all Joseph received was hate, but he moved on and kept dreaming anyway. This can be likened to what I call the "tennis ball rule:" If you take a tennis ball and go to the bottom of a pool and set it on the floor, as soon as you let go, it shoots up to the surface because, by its very nature it cannot remain at the bottom of the pool. So it is with an individual who is determined to get what he wants. Though he is taken to the bottom of the pool, he soon shoots up to the surface because he cannot, by his very nature, remain at the bottom.

And his brethren envied him; but his father observed the saying (Genesis 37:11)

However, always remember that though there will always be haters, there will also always be someone that will believe in you. Many times people disregard our goals, calling them pipe dreams and crackpot ideas, but there will always be someone who digests what you say and has confidence that you will accomplish it. In Joseph's case, his father rebuked him (probably to save face rather than to put him down) but he also observed what Joseph said because his father knew that there was something special about Joseph. Despite the negativity that surrounds us, we must open our eyes and hearts to those that give what we say some thought and wonder what it all means. We must always be able to find the good in the bad; as Robert Louis Stevenson said, "Don't judge each day by the harvest you reap but by the seeds you plant."

And the Lord was with Joseph, and he was a prosperous man (Genesis 39:2)

Genesis chapter 39 outlines the life of Joseph after he is sold to a band of Midianites. What is most striking in verse two is the use of the word *prosperous*. I do not know how happy I would be to be called prosperous when I have been hated, rebuked, thrown in a pit, sold to Midianites, and finally sold again to an Egyptian officer! The Hebrew word for prosperous in this case is *tsaleach*; pronounced *tsaw-lay-akh*[2]. It means, "to push forward." Therefore, Joseph had pushed forward; considering Egypt is the site where his two dreams would come true. Joseph's greatest advantage in this was that the Lord was with him.

And his master saw that the Lord was with him, and that the Lord made all that he did to prosper in his hand. And Joseph found grace in his sight, and he served him. And he made him overseer over his house, and all that he had he put into his hand (Genesis 39:3-4)

Though Joseph was now a slave, he served his master with all he had. This inward beauty soon began to resound in his physical being and in the quality of his work because "the Lord made all that he did to prosper in his hand." As we dream and begin to work towards our dreams, we will always meet people that need what we have and we must never neglect to serve them. All his life, he was pampered, spoiled and a brat; but once ushered into this new setting, he began to mature and learn that for him to succeed he would have to first learn how to serve.

You can have anything that you want if you only help enough other people get what they want – Zig Ziglar

Genesis chapter 40 outlines Joseph's life in prison after his master's wife wrongfully accuses him. The Bible says that Joseph "was a goodly person and well-favoured;" this means that Joseph was fine! This means that Joseph wasn't just all that and a bag of chips – he was the dip too! Potiphar's wife had an eye for him and tried to sleep with him but he refused. Genesis 39:12 says:

> And she caught him by his garment, saying, lie with me; and he left his garment in her hand, and fled, and got him out.

Although Joseph acted nobly and speedily by making a swift exit, a valuable lesson is illustrated…run, but never leave your garment! Take your clothes with you!

Despite Joseph's subsequent imprisonment, the Lord's favor was still upon him such that "the keeper of the prison committed to Joseph's hand all the prisoners that were in the prison" (Genesis 39:22) and "the keeper of the prison looked not to anything that was under his hand because the Lord was with him [Joseph] and that which he did, the Lord made it to prosper" (Genesis 39:23). Joseph continued to serve and when the king's butler and baker came under Joseph's care, he interpreted the dreams that each of them had. He only asked them to remember him when they were released from prison.

What lies as significant is the fact that it was not until two years had passed that Joseph's request to be remembered was met. It is from this point that Joseph began to steadily rise to power – after thirteen years of servitude!

You see, you can have anything that you want if you only help enough *other* people get what they want. Joseph helped his master Potiphar, the keeper of the prison, the butler, the baker and the king before his own dream came alive. "Give till it hurts. If people disappoint you, it's because they failed to see the bigger picture. Don't worry; your deeds of kindness will come back to you in the end," wrote S.B Fuller.

Dreamers are not only visionaries; they are also missionaries
– Kozhi Sidney Makai

You see, dreamers are not only visionaries – mapping out their lives with precision – they are also missionaries; serving everyone that they possibly can. Life is full of twists and turns but when you fail to realize your dream, don't give up the quest – just change your strategy and approach. Joseph, as a spoiled brat, must have thought that his grand dreams would be realized without thirteen years of service, being thrown in a pit, being sold into slavery, being wrongfully accused, and finally being thrown in prison. However, as a mature, virtuous and wise man, Joseph realized that he had to transcend adversity and work towards reaching his dream.

Dreaming: It means daring to reach, to climb, to crawl, to scratch, to get back up when you've been knocked down, to push forward – ever forward – to forgive. It means sacrificing everything, if necessary, to carve out a place for your own existence. It means living – Percy Sutton

Percy Sutton, lawyer-turned-politician, successful entrepreneur and owner of the famed Apollo Theater, hit the nail on the head when he said that dreaming means "daring to reach, to climb, to crawl, to scratch, to get back up when you've been knocked down, to push forward – ever forward – to forgive. It means sacrificing everything, if necessary, to carve out a place for your own existence. It means living." Joseph did all the above because he forgave his brethren and said, "Be not grieved, nor angry with yourselves, that ye sold me hither; for God did send me before you to preserve life" (Genesis 45:5).

I know that as you read this book, you have dreams that you think are not likely to ever become reality, but be assured that, as a Christian, the Lord is with you and HE has personally given you those dreams. You see, in biblical times, a dream was more than just a dream; many believed it was one way in which the supernatural world communicated with humans[3]. Indeed, some people desperately sought these revelations by sleeping in the temple or another holy place. Today, you and I do not have to be asleep for us to have dreams that God places in us for specific purposes. I know that you have some things that God has put in you that you need to follow through on but you must begin by believing in yourself and in the fact that God can and will use you if you afford Him the opportunity to do so.

NOTHING IS RANDOM: THERE IS DIVINE PURPOSE TO EVERYTHING

Joseph's life is an example of how a simple life can be taken and molded to perform a great and divine purpose. An excerpt from *Winter's Tale* by Mark Helprin reads:

> Nothing is random, nor will anything ever be, whether a long string of perfectly blue days that begin and end in golden dimness, the most seemingly chaotic political acts, the rise of a great city, the crystalline structure of a gem that has never seen the light, the distributions of fortune, what time the milkman gets up, the position of the electron, or the occurrence of one astonishingly frigid winter after another. Even electrons, supposedly the paragons of unpredictability, are tame and obsequious little creatures that rush around at the speed of light, going precisely where they are supposed to go. They make faint whistling sounds that when apprehended in varying combinations are as pleasant as the wind flying through a forest, and they do exactly as they are told. Of this, one can be certain. And yet there is a wonderful anarchy, in that the milkman chooses when to arise, the rat picks the tunnel into which he will dive when the subway comes rushing down the track from Borough Hall, and the snowflake will fall, as it will. How can this be? If

nothing is random, and everything is predetermined, how can there be free will? The answer to that is simple. Nothing is predetermined; it is determined, or was determined, or will be determined. No matter, it all happened at once, in less than an instant, and time was invented because we cannot comprehend in one glance the enormous and detailed canvas that we have been given – so we track it, in linear fashion, piece by piece. Time, however, can be easily overcome; not by chasing light, but by standing back far enough to see it all at once. The universe is still and complete. Everything that ever was, is; everything that ever will be, is - and so on, in all possible combinations. Though in perceiving it we imagine that it is in motion, and unfinished, it is quite finished and quite astonishingly beautiful. In the end, or rather, as things really are, any event, no matter how small, is intimately and sensibly tied to all others. All rivers run full to the sea; those who are apart are brought together; the lost ones are redeemed; the dead come back to life; the perfectly blue days that have begun and ended in golden dimness continue, immobile and accessible; and, when all is perceived in such a way as to obviate time, justice becomes apparent not as something that will be, but as something that is.

When God called Moses to service, He told him His name was "I AM THAT I AM." When Moses asked Him whom he would say sent him, the Lord responded, "Say unto the children of Israel, 'I AM hath sent me unto you.'" It may be quite peculiar that the present tense was used here but it must be also realized that God transcends time and space. Therefore, HE is behind all that takes place within and without time and space.

There is a divine call on your life. You picked up this book and that too is part of that divine structure and call. Realize that God is not a God of confusion but a God of peace. Chaos is what describes the world before God began His work on earth in Genesis chapter one.

97

God will always turn nothing into something simply by the power of His word. Just as Joseph was nothing before God began to train him and coach him, you too can be trained and coached to do the will of God and fulfill the purpose of Almighty God. Are you willing?

Know what your dreams will cost and be willing to pay the price - Bill Pinkney

As you set out to discover the dreams that you have, remember that you are the only one that can stop you from reaching and achieving your dreams. If Joseph could do it as a slave, you can do it. If Joseph could do it behind bars, you can most certainly do it too. Only believe; all things are possible...

Chapter Eleven

At all levels, education is the key to chisel away poverty. An education not only affects how you think but how you perceive your world
– Isaiah Thomas

The question to be asked at the end of an educational step is not 'what has the student learned?' but 'what has the student become?'
– James Monroe

Kozhi Sidney Makai

I have very fond memories of Lusaka West – the place I spent about eight years of my life before I moved to the United States. We had a community center we affectionately called "the council," which housed a mini resort and a bar. Standing at the bar one day, as I had often done, I came upon a poster as I ordered our soft drinks. It read:

GREAT MINDS

GREAT MINDS DISCUSS IDEAS.
ORDINARY MINDS DISCUSS EVENTS.
SIMPLE MINDS DISCUSS PEOPLE.
SO, WHERE DO YOU FIT IN?

As discussed in chapter two, the mind is a very powerful asset that each of us has been endowed with and what we do with it is what matters most. Everyone is educated in life in one way or another, whether at Harvard or in the School of Hard Knocks. Certainly, the education step of one's life is one of the most crucial.

The etymology of the word *education* is very interesting. The word education comes from the root word *educate*. Educate comes from the Latin words *educo*[1], *educatum*[2], and *eductum*[3] which mean "to lead forth[4]" or "to bring up a child[5]." "Educo[6]," however, is the primary root word and it means, "to lead out or lead forth[7];" "e" means *out*, and "duco" means *to lead*[8]. Therefore, Webster's Encyclopedic Dictionary defines *educate* as: "to cultivate and train the mental powers of; to instruct; to train; to rear" and *education* as: "the act of educating, teaching, or training; the act or art of developing and cultivating the various physical, intellectual, aesthetic, and moral faculties." From the above definitions, we see that education is ongoing and perpetual. Education leads us out of stasis and into an arena of life we have never experienced before. Whether or not the education is a formal one, it transforms us into new creatures with more to give.

'Tis education forms the common mind; just as the twig is bent the tree's inclined ~ Alexander Pope

100

Education affords us the opportunity to gain understanding, knowledge, insight, and wisdom. A fundamental theme of Old Testament wisdom literature, i.e. Proverbs, Job, Ecclesiastes, and the wisdom psalms, is that *the fear of the Lord is the beginning of knowledge and wisdom.* The book of Proverbs, perhaps the first biblical book I read as a child, is filled with wisdom. The word *proverb* has connotations with wisdom as stated in chapter one of Proverbs. Verses two through six answer the question: *What are proverbs for?*

> The purpose of these proverbs is to teach people wisdom and discipline, and to help them understand wise sayings. Through these proverbs, people will receive instruction in discipline, good conduct, and doing what is right, just, and fair. These proverbs will make the simple-minded clever. They will give knowledge and purpose to young people. Let those who are wise listen to these proverbs and become even wiser. And let those who understand receive guidance by exploring the depth of meaning in these proverbs, parables, wise sayings, and riddles – Proverbs 1:2-6, New Living Translation

In essence, wisdom can indeed be taught. Wisdom is a very valued asset in our twenty-first century world and was also, and perhaps even more, valued in the ancient world. Chapter two of Proverbs reiterates the importance of wisdom as it says,

> Happy is the person who finds wisdom and gains understanding. For the profit of wisdom is better than silver, and her wages are better than gold. Wisdom is more precious than rubies; nothing you desire can compare with her. She offers you life in her right hand, and riches and honor in her left. She will guide you down delightful paths; all her ways are satisfying. Wisdom is a tree of life to those who embrace her; happy are those who hold her tightly – Proverbs 2:13-18, New Living Translation

Proverbs 4:7 says that *wisdom is the principal thing.* It takes, for instance, wisdom to marry the right man or woman, raise a family, and maintain the family unit in times of trouble and turmoil. Surely, we all need wisdom. In this chapter we will look at the advantages and benefits that wisdom, understanding, insight, and knowledge – collectively gained through "education" – afford us as we embark on the journey towards success.

Formal education will make you a living. Self-education will make you a fortune – Dennis Kimbro

In today's competitive world, formal education is a significant predictor of how high a person will rise. Fortune 500 companies are not looking for high school graduates; they are looking for candidates who hold Masters degrees and doctorates. However, this should not be misconstrued as an idea that Masters and PhD degree holders are necessarily smarter than high school graduates. For example, my "surrogate" parents fired their ranch manager who is a graduate of the prestigious Texas A & M University. Though he has a degree in ranch management, he was not worth his salt as he failed to do simple tasks such as maintaining the cows in a specific pasture. As Dr. Kimbro wrote, *formal education will make you a living. Self-education will make you a fortune.*

Education is all about initiative and the hunger for wisdom and understanding. You can sit in class everyday and yet learn nothing because you are simply not interested. Wisdom, understanding, knowledge, and insight can be taught; it is up to you to discipline yourself to learn. It is such a shame when I hear men and women in their mid-thirties and forties wish they had paid a little more attention in school and taken their education more seriously. As a registration assistant at North Harris College, it pained me to see young people's freshman transcripts filled with "F's." What they fail to see is that this will always reflect upon their abilities.

Education leads to understanding, understanding leads to alternative solutions – Greg Smith

Watching *The Oprah Winfrey Show* one day, I was fascinated by her guest, Greg Smith. Greg Smith was, then, a 10-year-old college student, certainly in that positively deviant IQ section, who stated that *education leads to understanding, understanding leads to alternative solutions.* Clearly born with an intellectual gift, Greg acknowledged the fact that this was his gift from God and that he would strive to utilize it to its full potential. You see, education does lead to understanding. Understanding is simple insight that allows a person to have in – sight into things.

The principal goal of education is to create men [and women] who are capable of doing things, not simply of repeating what other generations have done – men [and women] who are creative, inventive and discoverers – Jean Piaget

In a world that is always looking for new things, novelty is a key ingredient in any successful endeavor nowadays. The purpose of education is to provide a window of opportunity to be and to do something novel. The French child development psychologist Jean Piaget stated a very important point when he stated that education's purpose is to *create.* As a college student, I could not stand having an instructor who did not create in me a desire to become more than what I already was.

In order for one to reach intellectual maturity, formal and self-education must be intertwined to produce a well-rounded individual. Too many preachers lack "secular" knowledge and, indeed, many businessmen lack scriptural and spiritual knowledge. This book has been made possible because I began to prepare for such an endeavor many, many months ago by collecting interesting stories, highlighting valuable studies and quotes as well as developing in my college career. Try it; you have no idea what you may be able to do with what you are preparing for. Remember: *Success occurs when opportunity meets preparation.*

THE SIX "P" THEORY OF SUCCESS

Prior preparation prevents poor pathetic performance
– Bruce Carroll

No other professor impacted the final year of my time at North Harris College more than professor Bruce Carroll. A rookie biology instructor at the time and graduate of Prairie View A & M University, this man really connected with me as I took biology with him. Biology, being a science, gave many of his students a tough time. However, this gentleman was very cordial and did all he could to assist us develop as young men and women. He went to the farthest lengths to ensure we grasped the information and got the grade.

However, to me, he did much more than that; he taught me about life. He taught us the reality of life outside the classroom although he understood that most of us were in his course to meet the science requirement for graduation. Thus, as he taught the material he likened it to the world of sports, social gatherings and business. In doing so, I believe that he taught me valuable lessons for a life outside the college environment.

I remember the lecture he gave us one afternoon after he revealed the grades of the first lecture exam. Many of us were discontent with our performance and, being the high achiever he is, he felt that our grades reflected on his teaching ability and quality. He said a lot of things to us that afternoon but the words that stuck in my mind were what I now affectionately call *The Six "P" Theory of Success*: **P**RIOR **P**REPARATION **P**REVENTS **P**OOR **P**ATHETIC **P**ERFORMANCE. Think about it: does this theory make sense or what? If we are prepared prior to an event, we prevent poor and pathetic performance — be it a decision needing to be made or conquering adversity.

Education is not preparation for life; education is life itself
~ John Dewey

Irrespective of the standard of education you have had, irrespective of the experience you have had in education, the responsibility to glean all that you can out of every learning opportunity is yours. We can long eternally for professors and teachers to be more interactive and easy-going with students, but the reality of life is that one's disposition and attitude towards the acquisition of wisdom and understanding is what matters in the end.

IS FORMAL EDUCATION FOR EVERYONE?

I quit college to start Dell Computer Corporation, and I don't regret that. But I would never advocate that young people today pass up an opportunity for higher education. Unless you have an idea that's very time-critical, it's always better to go to college if you can – Michael S. Dell

Anyone that has any knowledge of computers and the world of business will have heard of Michael S. Dell – the founder of Dell Computers. Dell Computer Corporation, headquartered in Austin, Texas, is the largest personal computer company in the world. Michael Dell started it out of his dorm room at the University of Texas at Austin some fifteen years ago. He is Chairman and CEO with a net worth in the $20 billion range and he isn't even 40 yet!

> The company was founded in 1984 on a simple concept: that by selling personal computer systems directly to customers, Dell could best understand their needs, and efficiently provide the most effective computing solutions to meet those needs.
>
> Dell holds the number two slot in worldwide market share and is consistently the leader in liquidity, profitability and growth among all major computer systems companies, with approximately 40,000 employees around the globe. The company ranks first in the United States, where it is the leading supplier of personal computers to business customers, government agencies, educational institutions and consumers.
>
> What's the catch? Michael Dell did *not* finish his degree at the University of Texas at Austin. "I quit college to start Dell Computer Corporation, and I don't regret that. But I would never advocate that young people today pass up an opportunity for higher education. Unless you have an idea that's very time-critical, it's always better to go to college if

105

you can," says Dell. How wisely put! It is my contention that though Dell did not finish college, he used everything else around him to increase in wisdom through "self-education." This manipulation of the resources around him allowed him to become the youngest CEO of a company ever to earn a ranking on the Fortune 500®. The company has been included on Fortune's list of "Most Admired Companies" since 1995, and in 1998, *Business Week* magazine named Dell as the "Best Performing Information Technology Company" in the world. Dell was also the top-performing stock among the *Standard & Poor's 500* and *NASDAQ* 100 in 1996 and 1997, and represented the top-performing U.S. stock on the Dow Jones World Stock Index. The value of Dell's stock has risen nearly 50,000 percent over the past decade, and in 1999, *The Wall Street Journal* named Dell No. 1 in total return to investors over the past three, five and ten years.

Because of the phenomenal success of the company, Michael Dell has been honored many times for his visionary leadership, earning the titles "2001 Chief Executive of the Year" by *Chief Executive* Magazine, "Entrepreneur of the Year" from *Inc.* magazine, "Man of the Year" by PC Magazine, "High Impact CEO" by executive search firm Heidrick and Struggles, "Top CEO in American Business" from Worth magazine and "CEO of the Year" by *Financial World* and *Industry Week* magazines. In 1997, 1998 and 1999, he was included in Business Week's list of "The Top 25 Managers of the Year." In addition, executive search firm Heidrick and Struggles named Michael their "High Impact CEO" for 1996 and 1997.[8]

This is an example of a man that has used the resources before him to improve himself and his station in life. You, too, have an opportunity to better yourself if you will realize that formal education is *not* the single key to a successful life. Indeed there are some that have, through formal education, become phenomenally successful but the bulk of the top CEO's have a combination of both formal and self-education. You must glean all that you can from the situations around you; that means you *will* have to pay more attention to the things around you.

WISDOM IS THE PRINCIPAL THING

I am convinced that wisdom is acquired by living purposefully and objectively. One must discipline and control oneself. Always keep yourself in a firm position to defend your integrity – Jake Simmons

What *is* wisdom? Why is it important? Why should I even bother with being wise? These, and questions like them, are questions that may be running through your mind right now. In a sentence, wisdom is the *principal* thing. The Hebrew word for "principal" is *reshiyth*[9] – pronounced *ray-sheeth*. This word is used only once (Proverbs 4:7) in the entire Bible and means "beginning[10]," "the first in order or rank[11]," or "chiefest[12]." It is used to signify that wisdom is the *foundation* upon which everything is made. Indeed, the words that called into being all that exists came from the wisdom of God. Wisdom must first be obtained in order for you to begin to build your empire of success. Jake Simmons, the first internationally successful black oilman, noted that wisdom is acquired by living both *purposefully* and *objectively*. A haphazard life and mind knows no wisdom…

A father, full of wisdom and understanding, was trying to get his children to understand the importance of wisdom. He said:

> Get wisdom, get understanding; forget it not; neither decline from the words of my mouth. Forsake her not, and she shall preserve thee; love her, and she shall keep thee. Wisdom is the principal thing; therefore get wisdom; and with all thy getting get understanding. Exalt her and she shall promote thee; she shall bring thee to honor, when thou dost embrace her. She shall

give to thine head an ornament of grace; a crown of
glory shall she deliver to thee. Proverbs 4:5-9

An education will afford you opportunities to grow and develop in
areas of your life that are significant. The Bible says God's Word <u>never</u>
returns void but accomplishes that unto which it was sent. God's
promise of wisdom's fruit is true and sincere, but you will reap the
benefits of wisdom only if you hunger and thirst after it.

Education is a progressive discovery of our own ignorance
~ Will Durant

Growing up on our farm in Lusaka, I learned very quickly that when
we sowed (a time I absolutely disliked, I should add) there was an
imminent harvest in the wake. Consequently, if you will sow into
wisdom by applying yourself to the disciplines required to attain it,
you will find good success in all your endeavors. Key to doing this is
the fact that – as Allan Oggs' book is entitled – *you've gotta have the want
to*!

LACK OF KNOWLEDGE = DESTRUCTION & CAPTIVITY

It seems rather harsh to say that the lack of knowledge leads to
destruction and captivity, but it is a biblical principal. In Hosea 4:6,
the Lord says, "My people are destroyed for lack of knowledge," and
in Isaiah 5:13, the Lord says, "Therefore my people are gone into
captivity because they have no knowledge."

Without wisdom you will fall into captivity and destruction, for
poverty is a mental disease that leads people into captivity and finally
into death – be it spiritual or physical. If you want to break a man,
first make it hard for him to simply feed, clothe and provide shelter
for his family and you will quickly tear him down. Having witnessed
poverty firsthand in my travels, I have come to conclude that lack of
knowledge does indeed lead to destruction and captivity.

The mind that is properly disciplined and directed to a clear-cut objective cannot be defeated - Kimbro

Without wisdom, success will not only be short lived, it will not be real. Education and wisdom are related in that education is the crucible in which wisdom is developed. Because it takes discipline to be educated, wisdom is not something that will come easily. Simply put, education is the doorway towards wisdom. Education will help you develop your knowledge base and therefore enhance your development and growth as an achiever. Do not, therefore, neglect education in any form – it will bring you great success!

Chapter Twelve

He who has never failed has never succeeded – Kimbro

Dr. John Maxwell of Injoy Stewardship Services has greatly influenced my life through his books, conferences and tape series. In his book, *Becoming a Person of Influence*, I read an inspirational testimony about rebounding from failure and destruction:

> Author Nena O'Neill once said, "Out of every crisis comes the chance to be reborn." The people of Enterprise, Alabama, understood that idea. In their town stands a monument to the Mexican boll weevil, erected in 1919. The story behind it is that in 1895, the insect destroyed the county's major crop – cotton. After that disaster, local farmers began to diversify, and the peanut crop of 1919 far exceeded the value of even the best ones comprised of cotton. On the monument are the following words: "In profound appreciation of the boll weevil and what it has done as the herald of prosperity...Out of a time of struggle and crisis has come new growth and success. Out of adversity has come blessing."

Failure is a natural component of success; indeed, we have all failed at one time or another. Think about it: did you hit the ball the first time you swung a baseball bat? And if you did, have you *always* hit it since? Not only is failure is a part of success, how we handle failure can determine whether or not we succeed.

You cannot measure an individual by his or her failures, but rather by what he or she makes of them - Kimbro

I finished high school when I was sixteen years old, after a successful high school career. I was named Best Sporting Student and was the captain of the basketball squad. I became a prefect and leader among students, and graduated in the top quarter of my class. Then I went to Evelyn Hone College and took Advanced Level math, chemistry and biology – and I failed them all! After encouragement from my parents that such shocking failure was only a minor setback, I set off for America with hopes of landing an athletic scholarship with the

University of Houston: I failed again. I returned to Zambia for a few months and then set off to Moscow, Russia for further studies but I failed again, miserably! Then I ventured to Johannesburg, South Africa where I landed a spot on the basketball team with Rand Afrikaans University along with my brother Francis. I hoped to land myself a pro deal in Johannesburg but I failed again! Finally, after praying for guidance and seeking my father's support for another move, after several months I returned to the United States and enrolled at North Harris College where I finally found success. During my second semester, I was awarded the North Harris College Outstanding Mathematics Student Award. In my second year, I was nominated and named to the National Dean's List and the College Board Talent Roster for Outstanding Transfer Students. All of this only goes to show that success and failure travel parallel; it is, however, up to us to work out the details.

It must be born in mind that failure to reach a goal is not tragic. The tragedy lies in not having a goal to reach
– Benjamin Mays

Many people have been unable to realize their dreams simply because they feared failing. However, it is more tragic to *not* have a goal than to fail to reach one. R.H. Macy failed seven times before his store in New York caught on. English novelist John Creasey got 753 rejection slips before he published 564 books. Babe Ruth struck out 1,330 times, but he also hit 714 home runs. You needn't worry about failure; worry, rather, about the chances you miss when you don't even try.

HOW WE FAIL

♦Refusing to enlist others to help us

Saying that we never know when we're going to fail is foolish, for at certain times, although we know that failure is imminent, we decide to go on – even against our better judgment. A major reason many people fail is their inability to enlist help when it is needed. A good illustration of this problem is the story of a bricklayer who got hurt at a building site. He was trying to get a load of bricks down from the top floor of a building without asking for help from anyone else. In his insurance claim, he wrote:

> It would have taken too long to carry all the bricks down by hand, so I decided to put them in a barrel and lower them by a pulley, which I had fastened to the top of the building. After tying the rope securely at ground level, I then went up to the top of the building; I fastened the rope around the barrel, loaded it with bricks, and swung it over the sidewalk for the descent. Then I went down to the sidewalk and untied the rope, holding it securely to guide the barrel down slowly. But since I weigh only 140 pounds, the 500-pound load jerked me from the ground so fast that I didn't have time to think of letting go of the rope. As I passed between the second and the third floors I met the barrel coming down. This accounts for the bruises and the lacerations on my upper body. I held tightly to the rope until I reached the top where my hand became jammed in the pulley. This accounts for my broken thumb. At the same time, however, the barrel hit the sidewalk with a bang and the bottom fell out. With the weight of the bricks gone, the barrel weighed only about 40 pounds. Thus my 140-pound body began a swift descent, and I met the empty barrel coming up. This accounts for my broken ankle. Slowed only slightly, I continued the descent and landed on the pile of brocks. This accounts for my sprained back and broken collarbone. At this point I lost my presence of mind completely, and I let go of the rope and the empty barrel came crashing down on me. This accounts for my head injuries. And as for the last question on your insurance form, "What would I do if the same situation rose again?" Please be advised I am finished trying to do the job all by myself.

Failure is, in a sense, the highway to success
– William Keats

We often fail because we fear appearing incompetent to peers but some situations call for us to enlist the help of others because failing alone – or facing calamity alone – is not a good feeling. I have traveled quite extensively, and one thing that can certainly be tough is sitting in a hotel room or an airport lobby alone, waiting. Ecclesiastes 4:9-12 says:

> Two people can accomplish more than twice as much as one; they get a better return for their labor. If one person falls, the other can reach out and help. But people who are alone when they fall are in real trouble. And on a cold night, two under the same blanket can gain warmth from each other. But how can one be warm alone? A person standing alone can be attacked and defeated, but two can stand back-to-back and conquer. Three are even better, for a triple-braided cord is not easily broken (New Living Translation)

It is essential, then, to ensure that certain paths of our journey to success be walked, not alone, but with company. Not all stages of the journey are profitable when walking alone, for some great calamity may befall you and you *will* need others to help you.

♦We refuse to play as part of the team

Team work can be a great asset to the success journey and in your come up. You must learn to appreciate the hands that hold you up as you climb the ladder, because they will be the ones to catch you should you slip and fall. I once read a story about a farmer who used to hitch up his old mule to a two-horse plow everyday and say, "Get up, Beauregard. Get up, Satchel. Get up, Robert. Get up, Betty Lou."

One day his neighbor, hearing the farmer, asked, "How many names does that mule have?"

"Oh, he has only one," answered the farmer. "His name is Pete. But I put blinders on him and call out all the other names so he will think other mules are working with him. He has a better attitude when he's part of a team."

You need to become part of some kind of team and enlist the assistance of others as you grow and develop into the man or woman of God you have been called to be. I am all about privacy and self-reliance but there are certain things that I simply cannot do on my own and I must ask for help. I cannot fly a plane so I enlist British Airways to take me to my destinations.

Chikwekwe chamwenda wika – A.A.M Makai

The above words are only some of the wisest that my late father, A.A.M Makai once told me. The direct translation being: *Although the hornbill tends to fly alone, there are always some behind him.* Be a hornbill, if you will, but always have some folks behind you.

FIVE LESSONS TO LEARN FROM GEESE[1]

Christine Hill published five lessons that can be learned from geese. I was really touched as I read them because she combines both the facts of the matter as well as the lesson to be learnt from each fact:

> **Fact 1**: As each goose flaps its wings it creates an "uplift" for the birds that follow. By flying in a "V" formation, the whole flock adds 71% greater flying range than if each bird flew alone.
> *Lesson 1*: People who share a common direction and sense of community can get where they are going quicker and easier because they are traveling on the thrust of one another.
>
> **Fact 2**: When a goose falls out of formation, it suddenly feels the drag and resistance of flying alone. It quickly moves back into formation to take advantage of the lifting power of the bird in front of it.
> *Lesson 2*: If we have as much common sense as a goose, we stay in formation with those headed where we want

to go. We are willing to accept their help and give our help to others.

Fact 3: When the lead goose tires, it rotates back into the formation and another goose flies to the point position.

Lesson 3: It pays to take turns doing the hard tasks and sharing leadership. As with geese, people are interdependent on each other's skills, capabilities, and unique arrangements of gifts, talents, or resources.

Fact 4: Geese flying in formation honk to encourage those up front to keep up their speed.

Lesson 4: We need to make sure our honking is encouraging. In groups where there is encouragement, the production is much greater. The power of encouragement (to stand by one's heart or core values and encourage the heart and core of others) is the quality of honking we seek.

Fact 5: When a goose gets sick, wounded, or shot down, two geese drop out of formation and follow it down to help protect it. They stay with it until it dies or is able to fly again. Then, they launch out with another formation or catch up with the flock.

Lesson 5: If we have as much sense as geese, we will stand by each other in difficult times as well as when we are strong.

♦We have major self-esteem problems

Mark Twain once wrote that a man cannot be comfortable without his own approval. Often we walk into situations already feeling defeated, certain that we will fail. Then, when we fail, we are not at all surprised! Perhaps we feel that by eliminating the surprise factor, we will deal with things much easier. This is a lie from the enemy! If we do not believe in ourselves when we begin a particular quest, it mars our fortunes even before we can set sail. We have no positive perspective of ourselves and decide, therefore, to die as the frog in the poem below:

*Positive Perspective*²

*Two frogs fell into a can of cream
Or so I've heard it told
The sides of the can were shiny and steep,
The cream was deep and cold
"Oh what's the use?" said No. 1,
"'Tis fate - no help's around -
Goodbye, my friend! Goodbye, sad world!"
And weeping still, he drowned.
But No. 2 of sterner stuff,
Dog-paddled in surprise
The while he wiped his creamy face
And dried his creamy eyes*

*"I'll swim awhile, at least," he said
Or so it has been said
"It wouldn't really help the world
If one more frog was dead."
An hour or two he kicked and swam
Not once he stopped to mutter
But kicked and swam, and swam and kicked,
Then hopped out, via butter*

Life is not peaches and crème, and we have all been dropped in the same can. Some decide to swim and exit via butter, while others give in and drown.

YOUR ATTITUDE TOWARDS FAILURE DETERMINES YOUR ALTITUDE TOWARDS SUCCESS

Chuck Swindoll, the Christian evangelist, once wrote a moving piece on attitude:

The longer I live, the more I realize the impact of attitude on life. Attitude to me is more important than facts. It is more important than the past, than education, than money, than circumstances, than failures, than successes, than what other people think or say, or do. It is more important than appearance, giftedness or skill. It will make or break a company, a church, and a home. The remarkable thing is, you have a choice everyday regarding the attitude you will embrace for that day. We cannot change our past...we cannot change the fact that people will act in a certain way. We cannot change the inevitable. The only thing we can do is play on the one string we have, and that is our attitude. I am convinced that life is ten percent what happens to me and ninety percent how I react to it. And so it is with you. You are in charge of your attitude.[3]

In his book, *A View from the Zoo*, Gary Richmond describes how a newborn giraffe learns its first lesson:

The mother giraffe lowers her head long enough to take a quick look. Then she positions herself directly over her calf. She waits for about a minute, and then she does the most unreasonable thing. She swings her long, pendulous leg outward and kicks her baby, so that it is sent sprawling head over heels. When it doesn't get up, the violent process is repeated over and over again. The struggle to rise is momentous. As the baby calf grows tired, the mother kicks it again to stimulate its efforts. Finally, the calf stands for the first time on its wobbly legs. Then the mother giraffe does the most remarkable thing. She kicks it off its feet again. Why? She wants it to remember how it got up. In the wild, baby giraffes must be able to get up as quickly as possible to stay with the herd, where there is safety. Lions, hyenas, leopards, and wild hunting dogs all enjoy young giraffes, and they'd get it too, if the mother didn't teach her calf to get up quickly and get with it.

The late Irving Stone understood this. He spent a lifetime studying greatness, writing novelized biographies of such men as Michelangelo, Vincent Van Gogh, Sigmund Freud, and Charles Darwin.

Stone was once asked if he had found a thread that runs through the lives of all these exceptional people. He said, "I write about people who sometime in their life have a vision or dream of something that should be accomplished and they go to work. They are beaten over the head, knocked down, vilified, and for years they get nowhere. But every time they're knocked down they stand up. You cannot destroy these people. And at the end of their lives they've accomplished some modest part of what they set out to do."

Without a struggle, there can be no progress – Frederick Douglas

"Without a struggle, there can be no progress," wrote Frederick Douglas. If we look through the annuls of history, we will see that every progressive act – be it independence from oppression or the building of a church or business – is preceded by and intertwined with struggle. Progress and struggle are unlikely bedfellows. Indeed, circumstances in which progress takes place without struggle are rare. Struggles take place with the sweet smell of progress in the wake, like the smell of rain on a hot summer day.

When the United States gained independence from Britain, there was a great struggle. When Zambia broke free of colonization by the British, there was a great struggle. When Nelson Mandela and black South Africa ushered out the inhuman regime of apartheid, there was a struggle, one that had Nelson Mandela locked in prison for 26 years. When we turn our lives around and become children of God, there is a struggle.

Struggles will always precede great feats but it is always up to us to stand tall and make it through those struggles because, as Albert Einstein once stated, "In the middle of difficulty lies opportunity."

119

I do not know where you are right now in your life. I do not know if you are working towards becoming more complete and prosperous. What I do know, however, is that though the storm may come, you can and will make it if you will work to see your problems from a higher perspective. You do not have to live in your spiritual, financial or social limbo anymore. You can and will make it if you will just understand that your struggle is only part of your success.

Difficulties are meant to rouse, not discourage – William Ellery Channing

William Ellery Channing made a wonderful point when he suggested that the difficulties we go through are not meant to discourage us but rather rouse us. I must admit that "facing difficulty but being roused" takes a lot of mental discipline but the fact still remains that it *can* be done. Remember: if you say you can, you can; if you say you cannot, you cannot.

RESISTANCE: THE KEY TO GROWTH

If you have ever worked out in any form or fashion, you may have noticed that it takes resistance to build muscles. The heavier the resistance (weights), the bigger the muscles grow. It takes more energy and strength to walk up a hill than it does to walk down a hill or a level road. What would life be if all we ever did was go downhill or travel level roads? First, we would not know what uphill was and second, we would not develop and grow. We would not be able to completely utilize the potential we have inside of us.

As a progressive and evolving being, man is where he is that he may learn that he may grow; and as he learns the spiritual lesson which any circumstance contains for him, it passes away and gives place to other circumstances – James Allen

Sometimes it takes me a long time to look at a problem I'm going through as a necessary spiritual lesson. To be honest, I'm not always really excited to be enduring the pain and frustration that negative circumstances usually cause. Sometimes I feel it would be good enough for me to just skip the lesson and get to growth.

As I look back at my life, I now see that the times when my wisdom and understanding grew to new levels, times when I got closer to becoming the person I long to be, were all surrounded by negative circumstances and struggle. The greatest growth you will ever have is going to come from overwhelming negative circumstances.

Writing in "Byways of Blessedness," James Allen is strong in his call for us to embrace our circumstances:

> Let a person rejoice when he is confronted with obstacles, for it means that he has reached the end of some particular line of indifference or folly, and is now called upon to summon up all his energy and intelligence in order to extricate himself, and to find a better way; that the powers within him are crying out for greater freedom, for enlarged exercise and scope. No situation can be difficult of itself; it is the lack of insight into its intricacies, and the want of wisdom in dealing with it, which give rise to the difficulty. Immeasurable, therefore, is the gain of a difficulty transcended.

Perhaps this explains why sometimes it seems I can't shake a particular problem, or I keep trying to "take care of it" and end up failing miserably. Instead of fighting circumstances, we need to jump in and gain the insight and wisdom to handle it. Thus we become ready for the next lesson – except we are stronger, both in spirit and in wisdom!

Emmet Fox once wrote,

> It is the Law that any difficulties that can come to you at any time, no matter what they are, must be exactly what you need most at the moment, to enable you to take the next step forward by overcoming them. The

121

only real misfortune, the only real tragedy, comes when
we suffer without learning the lesson.

In my travels and spiritual and personal growth, I have come to see that this
world is filled with only good times and bad times. Most of us only take
issue with the bad times. Because we have not learned the principle behind
growth, we have not seen the beauty of growth in its entirety. Rather, we have
embraced only the mundane and "peachy" aspects of life. Struggles are an
essential part of growth, as the birth process testifies to. Why should it come
as such a surprise that as the child grows, he or she must face tough times?

I Peter 4:12-13 says, "Beloved, think it not strange concerning the
fiery trial which is to try you, as though some strange thing happened unto
you. But rejoice, inasmuch as ye are partakers of Christ's sufferings; that,
when his glory shall be revealed, ye may be glad also with exceeding joy."
Like Peter's second century audience, we seem to think that we will not face
any trials but rather seek to go through life without obstacle or hindrance.

It is prudent for us to face the realities of life and see that
though the trials are present, we will overcome them if we will stand
tall and face them correctly.

*Circumstances don't make a man; they reveal him. Like
teabags, our real strength comes out when we get into hot water
– Dr. J. Allen Peterson*

The Myth of the Greener Grass is Dr. J. Allen Peterson's critically acclaimed
book that has touched millions of lives across the world including my
own. Circumstances are a great indicator of one's character and state of
mind. Only when teabags are dropped in hot water do they truly show
us what they can do. Until they are dropped in hot water, they only
have a reputation for making tea. So it is with us: until we are dropped
in hot water, we only have a reputation or potential to perform certain
tasks. Championship teams do not play championships games until
championship day because they are not yet in hot water in the regular
season. The BP Top Eight soccer tournament in Zambia allows the
competitors to play the game at a higher level than does the regular
season. If you want to watch some great basketball, watch the NBA

playoffs or the NCAA Sweet Sixteen. Why? Because, *only in such difficult circumstances* will you see a new level of the game played.

CIRCUMSTANCES DIFFERENTIATE CHARACTER AND REPUTATION

William Hersey Davis wrote an interesting piece differentiating character and reputation. It reads,

*The circumstances amid which you live
determine your reputation...
The truth you believe determines your character...*

*Reputation is what you are supposed to be
Character is what you are
Reputation is the photograph
Character is the face
Reputation comes over one from without
Character grows up from within
Reputation is what you have when you come to a
new community
Character is what you have when you go away
Your reputation is made in a moment
Your character is built in a lifetime
Your reputation is learned in an hour
Your character does not come to light for a
year...
Reputation grows like a mushroom
Character lasts like eternity...
Reputation makes you rich or makes you poor
Character makes you happy or makes you
miserable...
Reputation is what men say about you on your
tombstone
Character is what the angels say about you
before the throne of God*

From this piece I realized that the way circumstances are presented to us determines what we build — either our character or our reputation. It is sad to note that a lot of what we do in life is determined more by our reputation than by our character. People end up making major judgments and decisions on reputation rather than character.

James Allen has inspired me greatly, and also many other writers and orators, because of his analysis of life and circumstances as part of our thought processes. Indeed, most of our problems and struggles tend to get our heads but we fail to realize that most times we cause those circumstances by our thought. He wrote,

> A person is the causer (though nearly always unconsciously) of his circumstances, and that, whilst aiming at the good end, he is continually frustrating its accomplishment by encouraging thoughts and desires which cannot possibly harmonize with that end.

As an example, Allen uses a rich man who is the victim of a painful and persistent disease as the result of gluttony. He's willing to give large sums of money to get rid of the disease and he fully expects that will be the cure. However, he never addresses the gluttonous desire that is the cause of his condition. He can never achieve good health because his desires are not in harmony with the good health he seeks, regardless of the money he spends.

So it is with us many times. We try very hard to get past the struggles we are facing but cannot possibly do so because our thoughts are messed up — we've got stinking thinking! Our thoughts must always be in harmony with our actions and also desires to see a particular end. Always let your character, not your reputation, be the guide and light in your life.

Conclusion

Now that we have come to the conclusion of what I hope is a tool and resource you can always return to, I would like to close by sharing with you William Arthur Wood's brilliant piece called forgetting yourself into greatness:

If you are wise, you will forget yourself unto greatness. Forget your rights, but remember your responsibilities. Forget your inconveniences, but remember your blessings. Forget your own accomplishments, but remember your debts to others. Forget your privileges, but remember your obligations. Follow the examples of Florence Nightingale, of Albert Schweitzer, of Abraham Lincoln, of Tom Dooley, and forget yourself into greatness.

If you are wise, you will empty yourself into adventure. Remember the words of General Douglas MacArthur: "There is not security on this earth. There is only opportunity." Empty your days of the search for security; fill them with a passion for service. Empty your hours of the ambition for recognition; fill them with the aspiration for achievement. Empty your moments of the need for entertainment; fill them with the quest for creativity.

If you are wise, you will lose yourself into immortality. Lose your cynicism. Lose your doubts. Lose your fears. Lose your anxiety. Lose your unbelief. Remember these truths: A son must soon forget himself to be long remembered. He must empty himself in order to discover a fuller self. He must lose himself to find himself.

Forget yourself into greatness. Empty yourself into adventure. Lose yourself into immortality.

It is harder to take action when we do not know we are in a rut than when we know. For some, this book has inspired them to go beyond the limitations they have inflicted on themselves or the limitations men have placed on them; for others, it has opened their eyes to some of the many possibilities they can use to better their lives. Above all, I hope that the greatest investment you have made is to place all your money in Jesus Christ stocks and bonds – with Him, you will never go wrong.

𝕹𝖔𝖙𝖊𝖘

CHAPTER 1 ♦ The Seed and the Fruit
The System and Order for Success

1. James Strong, *A Concise Dictionary of the Words in the Hebrew Bible* (Nashville, TN: Abingdon Press, 1890), pp. 116
2. The New Webster Encyclopedic Dictionary of the English Language: 1980 Edition, pp. 837
3. *Ibid.*, pp.669
4. James Strong, *A Concise Dictionary of the Words in the Hebrew Bible* (Nashville, TN: Abingdon Press, 1890), pp. 24
5. Dr. Creflo Dollar, *The Blessing* Tape Series (Creflo Dollar Ministries, 2001)
6. The New Webster Encyclopedic Dictionary of the English Language: 1980 Edition, pp. 760
7. Dr. Creflo Dollar, *The Blessing* Tape Series (Creflo Dollar Ministries, 2001)
8. The New Webster Encyclopedic Dictionary of the English Language: 1980 Edition, pp. 471
9. *Ibid.*, pp. 351
10. *Ibid.*, pp. 553
11. *Ibid.*, pp. 712
12. *Ibid.*, pp. 834
13. *Ibid.*, pp. 259

CHAPTER 2 ♦ Your Mind
The Field in which Seeds are Planted

1. Anonymous
2. Dennis Kimbro, *What Makes the Great Great* (New York, NY: Doubleday), pp. 101-140.
3. James Strong, *A Concise Dictionary of the Words in the Greek Testament* (Nashville, TN: Abingdon Press, 1890), pp. 11
4. The New Webster Encyclopedic Dictionary of the English Language: 1980 Edition, pp. 2

5. *Ibid.*, pp. 2
6. *Ibid.*, pp. 855
7. Francis Frangipane, *The Three Battlegrounds* (Cedar Rapids, IA: Arrow Publications, Incorporated, 1989), pp. 11-50.
8. From a personal email forward

CHAPTER 3 ♦ Your Attitude
The Gauge of Your Come Up

1. Anonymous
2. Yahoo! Education Encyclopedia Reference Section. Available online at http://education.yahoo.com/reference/encyclopedia/entry?id=24839
3. This is a concept adopted from John Maxwell in his teaching tape *Eleven Keys to Excellence*
4. James Strong, *A Concise Dictionary of the Words in the Hebrew Bible* (Nashville, TN: Abingdon Press, 1890), pp. 54

CHAPTER 4 ♦ Your Character
The Issues that Define You

1. Reader's Digest *Who's Who in the Bible: An Illustrated Biographical Dictionary* (Pleasantville, NY: Reader's Digest Association, Inc., 1994), pp. 68
2. *Ibid.*, pp. 68
3. Barry L. Bandstra, *Reading the Old Testament* (Albany, NY: Wadsworth Publishing Company, 1999), pp. 465
4. Stephen Carter, *Integrity* (New York, NY: HarperCollins Books, 1996), pp. 7

CHAPTER 5 ♦ Imitation
The Thief of Progress

1. Zig Ziglar, *Goals* (New York, NY: Simon & Schuster, 2000)
2. Bishop T.D Jakes, Manpower 1998 (Dallas, TX: TD Jakes Ministries, 1998)

CHAPTER 6 ♦ Ideas & Imagination
The Raw Materials for Achievement

1. The New Webster Encyclopedic Dictionary of the English Language: 1980 Edition, pp. 422
2. *Ibid*, pp. 422
3. *Ibid*, pp. 422

CHAPTER 7 ♦ Courage
Propelling Yourself Into Greatness

1. John Maxwell, *Becoming a Person of Influence* (Nashville, TN: Thomas Nelson Publishers, 1997), pp. 65
2. From a personal email forward
3. Author unknown at time of publication

CHAPTER 8 ♦ Desire
The Smoldered Fire of Achievement

1. John C. Maxwell, Failing Forward (Nashville, TN: Thomas Nelson Publishers, 2000), Cover

CHAPTER 9 ♦ Discipline
The Great Key to Success

1. The New Webster Encyclopedic Dictionary of the English Language: 1980 Edition, pp. 662
2. *Ibid*, pp. 662
3. *Ibid*, pp. 662
4. *Ibid*, pp. 662

CHAPTER 10 ♦ Dreams
Previews to Success

1. "Everybody has a dream" by Virginia Satir. Available online from Inspirational Stories at http://www.inspirationalstories.com/2/255.html

2. James Strong, *A Concise Dictionary of the Words in the Hebrew Bible* (Nashville, TN: Abingdon Press, 1890), pp. 99
3. Reader's Digest *Who's Who in the Bible: An Illustrated Biographical Dictionary* (Pleasantville, NY: Reader's Digest Association, Inc., 1994), pp. 243

CHAPTER 11 ♦ Education
The Tool That Chisels Away Poverty

1. The New Webster Encyclopedic Dictionary of the English Language: 1980 Edition, pp. 276
2. *Ibid*, pp 276
3. *Ibid*, pp 276
4. *Ibid*, pp 276
5. *Ibid*, pp 276
6. *Ibid*, pp 276
7. *Ibid*, pp 276
8. Available online from http://company.monster.com.hk/dellhk/
9. James Strong, *A Concise Dictionary of the Words in the Hebrew Bible* (Nashville, TN: Abingdon Press, 1890), pp. 106
10. *Ibid*, pp 106
11. *Ibid*, pp 106
12. *Ibid*, pp 106

CHAPTER 12 ♦ Failure
The Highway to Success

1. "Canada Geese – A lesson in team building," by Rick Hallson. Available online from Rick Hallson Seminars at http://www.rickhallson.com/index_files/rickhallsonteambuilding.htm
2. Anonymous
3. Received via email (no source available at time of publication)

About the Author

Kozhi Sidney Makai is a well-traveled and international inspirational speaker, Bible teacher, and founder of Spiritworx International. He has made teaching people how to live within and above their potential his life's mission. He holds a Bachelor's degree in Speech Communication and Psychology, a Master's degree in Business Communication with a specialization in Leadership & Influence, and is currently working on his Doctorate degree in Applied Management & Decision Sciences with a specialization in Leadership and Organizational Change. He is Adjunct Professor of Speech at North Harris College and also Communication Faculty at the University of Phoenix. As a writer, speaker, and "citizen of world," Kozhi travels the world sharing a message of higher level living. He lives in The Woodlands, Texas with his wife, Annie.

Printed in the United States
46509LVS00007B/103-153